CORNWALL COUNTY COUNCIL
LIBRARIES AND ARTS DEPARTMENT

ONE AND ALL

THE PEOPLE'S PRINCESS
A Portrait of H.R.H. Princess Mary, Duchess of Teck

by S. W. Jackman

© S. W. Jackman 1984

British Library Cataloguing in Publication Data.

Jackman, S. W.

The people's princess: a portrait of
H.R.H. Princess Mary, Duchess of Teck.
1. Mary, *Princess, Duchess of Teck*   2. Great
Britain — Princes and princesses — Biography

I. Title

941.081'092'4   DA559.M/

ISBN 0-946041-19-9

**Published by The Kensal Press,
Shooters Lodge, Windsor Forest, Berks.**

Printed and bound in Great Britain by
Hollen Street Press, Slough.
Typeset by Tek, England.

941.081
MAR

To Gloria, Ted and John
with affectionate regards

Acknowledgements

I wish to acknowledge the gracious permission of Her Majesty The Queen, Her Majesty the Queen of the Netherlands and Her Majesty the Queen of Denmark for the use of illustrative material in their collections. I am indebted to Mr John Murray and to the Longman Group for their kind permission to use items selected from works published by them. Acknowledgement is also due to The Illustrated London News Picture Library. Friends have been very generous in making photographs available to me from their private archives and albums and I am most appreciative of their generosity.

I wish to express my thanks to The University of Victoria Research and Travel Fund for aiding in my research. Dr John Duder was a most able and imaginative research associate and without his help the book could not have been written. Dinah Dickie coped with the manuscript, and various other individuals offered help and advice, in particular Rayner Unwin, Coenraad Tasee, Kees Willems, Duke Christian of Oldenburg, David Somerset, Prince Moritz of Hesse, Lord Napier, Lord Norwich and Geoffrey Skelsey. To all of these people I wish to say thank you. Mrs Millan and her colleagues of the Kensal Press have been very generous and helpful during all of the production of the book. I am also indebted to the Master and Fellows of Trinity Hall for their kind hospitality; over the years they have been most welcoming and I wish to acknowledge my appreciation of their generosity.

S.W.J.

University of Victoria, Victoria, B.C.
Trinity Hall, Cambridge.

Contents

List of Illustrations

The family of H.R.H. The Duke of Cambridge. From left to right The Duchess of Cambridge, The Duke of Cambridge, Frederick (Grand Duke of Mecklenburg–Strelitz, Augusta (Grand Duchess of Mecklenburg–Strelitz), Princess Mary and Prince George.

(From Kinloch Cooke — courtesy John Murray)

H.M. Augusta, Queen of Prussia, and later German Empress, was one of the many royal relations who had concerned herself about Princess Mary's marital prospects. After the Austro-Prussian War the intimacy of Augusta and the Cambridges and the Tecks went into a decline but later they became friends anew and met on visits to England and Germany.
(Lithograph by G. Fechter)

H.R.H. Adolphus Frederick, Grand Duke of Mecklenburg-Strelitz from 1904 to 1914, was the nephew of Princess Mary. He was called 'Doppus' by the family.
(Collection Staatsarchiv Schwerin)

CHAPTER ONE

Last of the Old Royals

In early December 1833, the Landgravine of Hesse-Homburg was seated at her desk in the Schloss busily engaged with her correspondence. To a friend in England she wrote 'Thank God my dearest Adolphus' mind is at ease about the Duchess of Cambridge, she has given him another little girl...' The latter was her niece, Mary Adelaide Wilhelmina Elizabeth, born on 27th November. The infant princess was the last of those to be born who properly can be considered true members of 'the old royal family'.

In the middle of the last century when the average person spoke about 'the royal family' it generally referred to Queen Victoria, Prince Albert and their children. However, to the cognoscenti 'the royal family' was composed of two parts. The first did, indeed, mean the reigning sovereign and her family, the second being designated 'the old royal family'. The latter did not mean the House of Stuart as might be imagined but rather it was composed of those princes and princesses who emphasized their connection with the House of Hanover rather than the House of Saxe-Coburg. Members of 'the old royal family' took vast pride in being known as Princes and Princesses of Great Britain and held that designations such as Prince George of Cumberland or Prince George of Cambridge were both novel and improper. Princess Augusta, the older sister of Princess Mary, never liked being known as 'of Cambridge' and was displeased to have 'the Father's title for a *family* name' and thought it 'perfectly wrong'. In one sense she was quite correct for the Act of Settlement of 1701 had declared that the descendants of the Electress Sophia should be called 'of Great Britain'. The 'old royal family' were inclined to believe the emphasis on the newer usage was somehow part of a plot adopted by Queen

Victoria and her consort, aided and abetted by King Leopold of the Belgians, to enhance the Saxe-Coburgs at the expense of their English relations. Yet, despite the feelings of some members of 'the old royal family' on the matter, the use of 'the Father's title for a *family* name' was accepted practice by the time of Princess Mary's birth in 1833. While being referred to as Princess Mary of Cambridge for the next three decades she never failed to emphasize her connections with 'the old royal family'.

When Princess Mary was born, eight of the fifteen children of King George III and Queen Charlotte still survived. There were four stout elderly princesses: Augusta and Sophia, who were spinsters; Mary, married to her cousin the Duke of Gloucester; and Elizabeth, the wife of the Landgraf of Hesse-Homburg. The first three lived in England, the Landgravine resided in Germany.

The eldest of the surviving sons was King William IV. He was aged sixty-four, not particularly clever, inclined to obstinacy and with a 'quarter-deck temper' which tended to erupt when he felt crossed over matters relating to his rank or his authority. When he became king he had a reputation for having liberal principles in contrast to those of his late brother, King George IV, but such was not really the case. At heart he was conservative and a traditionalist. He had married Princess Adelaide of Saxe-Meiningen in 1818, a rather plain and pious individual – prior to this he had lived for a number of years with Mrs Jordan by whom he had ten children. And while the much younger wife and the elderly husband were happy enough their two daughters both died as infants.

The next surviving son of George III was Ernest, Duke of Cumberland. If King William IV was relatively popular, the Duke was regarded in quite the reverse fashion. The public believed him to be a reactionary and a martinet whose influence on his brothers was pernicious. He was accused of having had an incestuous relationship with his sister, Princess Sophia, and no woman's virtue was safe in his company. He was thought to have murdered his valet and to be capable of the

H.R.H. Princess Mary, Duchess of Gloucester, was a daughter of King George III and the wife of her cousin H.R.H. Prince William, Duke of Gloucester. 'Minny', as the Princess was called in the family, was the favourite relation of all the Cambridges.
(Portrait by an unknown artist)

H.R.H. Prince Adolphus, Duke of Cambridge, father of Princess Mary, circa 1840. The drawing is by James Swinton and was thought by family to be an excellent likeness.
(From Kinloch Cooke — courtesy John Murray)

most heinous of crimes without a qualm. He was probably the most unpopular individual in Great Britain. His wife was Princess Frederica of Mecklenburg-Schwerin and, like her husband, she had a bad reputation. It was only the result of malicious gossip but she was never officially received by her mother-in-law or her husband's sisters. The Cumberlands had one son who was born in 1819 and called George.

The two youngest of the king's brothers were the Dukes of Sussex and Cambridge. The former was innocuous and amiable. He was an enthusiastic bibliophile and a mild Whig in politics. He was twice married but since he had not complied with the provisions of the Royal Marriage Act, neither of his so-called 'wives' were given royal rank. He had a son and daughter by his first marriage. His first wife took the title of Countess d'Ameland while the second was created a duchess in her own right by Queen Victoria. The Duchess Inverness, as she was called, was treated by everyone as a member of the family and after her husband's death lived for years in Kensington Palace. Adolphus Duke of Cambridge was the least objectionable of all George III's sons. He led a blameless life, was happily married and had three children.

Adolphus Frederick, Duke of Cambridge, was the tenth child and seventh son of George III. He was born on 24th February 1774, one year after his brother Augustus. As an infant he resided at Windsor but when he was about seven, he joined his brothers Ernest and Augustus at Kew where they were supervised by a couple of tutors and only paid occasional visits by their parents. When he was twelve, he was sent to live in Göttingen. King George III wanted to ensure that the Hanoverian connection was maintained by his family and also, more practically, he wished his sons to be proficient in German. When Adolphus arrived, his brothers were already in residence and the three youths appear to have made a good impression on everyone. The princes behaved in an exemplary fashion, lived modestly and quietly and seemed to be interested in their studies. Their father observed 'My accounts from Göttingen of the little colony I have sent there is very favourable,' and he added that his youngest son seemed to be extremely popular noting 'which from his lively manners is natural'.

Although assiduous enough as a student, Prince Adolphus really wanted to be a soldier and to emulate the career of his elder brother Frederick Duke of York. He was given a commission in the Hanoverian army and sent off to Berlin to learn his trade; after a few months he joined the British army as part of the Flanders campaign against the French. The whole expedition was appallingly badly organized and a disaster. During the campaign Prince Adolphus was wounded and invalided home to England where he was welcomed by his parents and sisters as a hero. After a few months, he was back under arms but this time served in the Hanoverian Corps under General Walmoden. The latter was his great-uncle, being a son of George II and his mistress Lady Yarmouth. The young officer's career with the Hanoverians ended when the corps withdrew from The Netherlands and returned to Germany.

Although still technically a serving soldier with the rank of Major-General, he now resumed his studies at the university. Everyone appears to have liked him and he was able 'to impress the Hanoverians with the superior charms of English gentlemen'; his conversation was 'fluent, various and entertaining'. This youthful paragon was his father's favourite son – George III liked his children when young and only became irritated and unhappy with them when they became adult and were no longer dependent upon him. He never seems to have quarrelled with his parents and remained on good terms with all his brothers and sisters. Even his eldest brother, who was notoriously mercurial in his attachments, always spoke well of his youngest brother and consistently showed him affection. Moreover, and this may be an indication of the fact that he never was embroiled with his relations, Prince Adolphus seems to have escaped attack by the press and the satirists. For the next few years his life was uneventful and he occupied himself with garrison duties.

When he was twenty-seven he was created Duke of Cambridge. The Dukedom had special associations with the House of Hanover, it being the title bestowed by Queen Anne on her successor, later George I. In 1803 he returned to England and having transferred from the Hanoverian army in which he had previously served, he was now a member of a British regiment. His martial activity was limited, chiefly being ceremonial or parade-ground, and he saw no active service during the final years of the war against France.

With the abdication of the Emperor Napoleon and the meeting of the diplomats in Vienna, the Electorate of Hanover was transformed into a kingdom and the Duke of Cambridge was sent over by the Prince Regent to be the Governor-general. The Duke of Cumberland, who was directly involved in the liberation of Hanover from the French, had hoped for the post but the Liverpool government had not been favourably inclined nor was the Prince Regent. The latter wanted a ruler who would be amenable to his personal inclinations and he felt that his brother Ernest was too independent-minded. Upon the Duke of Cambridge's arrival all the latent support from the Hanoverians for their sovereign was revived and he was given an enthusiastic welcome by the populace. He was so touched by his reception that he burst into tears. Upon accepting his new positon he had hoped that his arrival would be the harbinger of a more liberal regime but he was too sanguine in his anticipations. His powers were severely curtailed largely through the machinations of Count Münster who was exceedingly conservative and who held the post of Hanoverian envoy in London. The Prince Regent preferred the counsel of the Count to the advice proffered by his brother. The latter did finally manage to persuade the Regent of the need for some modest alterations in the mode of government and these were made in 1819. Not until 1831, however, was a proper liberal and constitutional regime established and this was to be short-lived, being abrogated in 1837 upon the accession of the Duke of Cumberland to the Hanoverian kingdom.

Deprived of real political power the Governor-general had to content himself with other aspects of his position. He made some name for himself as patron of the arts, was assiduous in his support of the musical talent in Hanover and attended the opera frequently. Like his father he set an excellent example in his domestic establishment; indeed his household was a model of propriety, a marked contrast to the rather raffish ménage of the Prince Regent at the Royal Pavilion in Brighton. All that was lacking was a suitable chatelaine but the Duke seemed quite content to remain a bachelor. He appears to have found purely masculine company agreeable and had no inclination to establish even an informal liaison to provide himself with feminine companionship. However, this way of life was to terminate with the death of his niece Princess Charlotte.

Despite the fact that George III had a large family, his only legitimate grandchild was the daughter of the Prince of Wales. She had married Prince Leopold of Saxe-Coburg in 1816 and died in childbirth the following year. The question of the succession to the throne now became an urgent one. The Prince of Wales, the Duke of York and the Duke of Cumberland were married, the remaining male members of the royal family were still legally unwed. The Dukes of Kent, Clarence and Sussex at various times lived with mistresses and in all cases there were children, but they were ineligible to succeed to the crown. The Duke of Cambridge who was by now forty-three and pre-eminently respectable was the most logical of the princes to ensure the succession. He had a good character, was an agreeable man and would be an ideal husband; he was an excellent prospect for any of the numerous German ruling dynasties seeking to promote an alliance between themselves and the British reigning family.

Actually his possible excursion into the matrimonial state was not the first that he had contemplated. Two decades previously he had been engaged to the widowed Princess Frederica of Prussia – she was the daughter of the Duke of Mecklenburg-Schwerin and sister of Queen Louisa of Prussia. The Duke had six daughters and with the exception of the

Queen of Prussia none of them had particularly good reputations but this did not deter her British suitor. Although a widow and a mother, she was young and attractive and his parents approved of his choice but were cautious and hesitant in setting a date for the marriage. Much to their shock and chagrin just when the formal consent was given the prospective bride broke the engagement and married the Prince of Solms-Braunfels. She had become his mistress after her fiancé had left Berlin and when she discovered she was pregnant she had consulted her sister the Queen of Prussia who suggested that she marry her lover. On learning that the Princess had wed another – they did not know the reason for her sudden decision – King George and Queen Charlotte were furious. They felt that Princess Frederica had insulted them. To add to their chagrin, she had jilted a Prince of Great Britain for a minor and insignificant German princeling.

The rejected suitor seems to have accepted the situation more philosophically and made no notable protest. Very probably he had not been in love with the Princess and may well have been jockeyed into proposing by her Prussian relations while he was serving in Berlin. Moreover, he had quite likely only contemplated matrimony out of a sense of duty to his parents and his country. There is no evidence that he bore a grudge against his erstwhile fiancée and was amiable enough to her when some years later she married his brother Ernest after being widowed a second time. Indeed, the correctness of his conduct to Princess Frederica was in marked contrast to that of his mother and his sisters who declined to receive her when she came to London. Having done the right thing by contemplating matrimony and taking the steps of actually becoming engaged and then having it broken off, he presumably felt that was all that was required of him. A bachelor life was quite agreeable and he saw no reason to change it. Events at Claremont forced him to reconsider his position.

Once confronted with the problem he was prepared to do what was understood to be his duty. The Regent's daughter had scarcely been buried when the Duke of Cambridge took the plunge and proposed to Princess Augusta, the youngest daughter of the Landgraf of Hesse. Her family were of suitable rank and importance, properly protestant – the House of Hesse was proud to claim as an ancestor Philip the Magnanimous the protector of Luther – and generally of a respectable character. The Landgraf was delighted and promptly accepted on behalf of his daughter. The prospective bridegroom observed, 'I really believe that on the surface of the globe there does not exist so happy a Being as myself. Every hour I feel that my esteem and attachment for my bride increases and she is really everything both as to heart, mind and Person that I would wish.' No ardent suitor could have expressed it better but considering the fact that he was only slightly acquainted with the lady in question such effusions of sentiment may seem a bit odd. However, the Duke of Cambridge was not a complicated individual, and, having made up his mind to marry, he was equally determined to be in love with his future wife. Indeed, a later observer of the ducal pair noted the union from the very beginning was one of perfect harmony and great affection. Princess Augusta's feelings are not recorded; princesses were expected to make suitable dynastic alliances and love played a small part in the matter. A future of some brilliance awaited the Hessian princess and life could not fail to be exciting for her as the Duchess of Cambridge. While her future husband was not a reigning prince nor the direct heir to the throne he was close enough to the succession to make it a possibility. In addition, to be a Princess of Great Britain had infinitely more cachet than that which accrued to the petty sovereigns in her own country.

Princess Augusta was not a raving beauty; she had 'a heavy, rather coarse face, and thick black eyebrows which gave her what her niece Victoria called "a severity of expression" '. In a miniature painted about the time of her marriage by Chalon she looks rather proud and haughty; she had a very definite view of the world and was much concerned to ensure the deference due to her because of her rank and position. Indeed, numerous of her contemporaries among the minor

A copy of a miniature of H.R.H. The Duchess of Cambridge, the mother of Princess Mary. The original was painted about the time of the Princess's marriage. Undoubtedly it is a highly flattering portrait but very typical in style of similar pictures of the 1820s.
(From a copy in a private collection)

Queen Adelaide, wife of King William IV, was one of Princess Mary's favourite aunts. Queen Adelaide was a charming woman and managed with great skill to get on with her rather difficult British relations.
(After a photographic copy in a private collection)

German princely families were almost passionate in maintaining their pretentious and subtle differences between serene highnesses and highnesses, ascertaining the number of guns fired in salute to mediatized and reigning families occupied the time of many royal personages. By no stretch of the imagination could Princess Augusta be considered well educated but she was quick and perceptive and was thought by her contemporaries 'to be clever'.

The wedding took place on 7th May 1818 in Cassel; following the ceremony the bride and the groom accompanied by her father immediately departed for England. The trip took about three weeks; the Channel crossing was exceedingly unpleasant and both the bride and her elderly father were very seasick. The recollection of this sea voyage remained engraved upon her mind and thereafter she approached the passage from Calais to Dover with dread.

In order to recover the royal party spent the night in Dover before proceeding to London. Everywhere the Cambridges were greeted with cordiality but the Duchess could hardly respond with enthusiasm as she was still feeling the effects of her seasickness. Once in London, preparations were immediately made for a second nuptial ceremony to be performed in the presence of the groom's family. The popular enthusiasm for the newly-weds continued unabated and wherever they went they were mobbed. Princess Augusta and her father soon discovered that the vociferous Londoners were far less restrained in showing their sentiments than were the stolid Germans.

After a summer in England the Duke and Duchess returned to Germany; to get back to the continent once more the Duchess had to face the horror of a Channel crossing but this time the sea was quite calm. Once in Hanover they were in a world and in a society they both enjoyed, and taking up residence in the viceregal palace for the winter and spending the summer at Villa Monbrillant nearby they established a pattern of life for the next two decades. Since the Duke had only the most limited of political powers he and his wife continued to emphasize the ceremonial role which he had adopted upon his appointment. One aspect of life which they cultivated was to participate in the numerous cultural and social activities organized by the citizens of Hanover. The arts in general enjoyed the active patronage of the viceregal pair. However, in contrast to the degree of ceremony in their public life, in private they revelled in cozy domesticity much as Queen Victoria and Prince Albert were to do many years later. In 1819 their first child, a son, was born and he was christened George after his grandfather and uncle. For a very short time the infant was heir to both the British and Hanoverian crowns but he was to be displaced in the former by his cousin Princess Victoria of Kent and in the latter by another cousin Prince George of Cumberland. Three years after the birth of Prince George, the couple had a second child, a daughter, whom they named Augusta after her mother and great-aunt. To most observers it would seem that there were unlikely to be any further additions to the family.

Upon his accession in 1820, George IV announced that he intended to visit Scotland, Ireland and Hanover. No British sovereign had been to Scotland since the seventeenth century and on that occasion Charles II was virtually a prisoner of the Covenanters and hardly a free agent. Ireland had been last visited by an English king at the Battle of the Boyne, and while Hanover was perhaps more fortunate since George II made frequent excursions to his German home and even died in the country, after 1760 the electorate and later kingdom had to make do with younger members of the reigning family. In fact it was some eighty years since the Hanoverians had seen their sovereign. George IV kept his promise and toured his German domain; however, the royal tour did not bring any announcement of an enhancement of the Duke of Cambridge's authority as had been hoped – and this despite the fact that King George IV had it forcibly indicated to him how difficult it was to administer Hanover with all the effective power in London. Count Münster's conservative policies were to continue to prevail and the minister's rather baleful

George and Augusta, the brother and sister of Princess Mary. The picture was probably painted in Hanover where their parents were residing.
(Courtesy Longman Group)

influence determined state policy. The visit of the sovereign had delighted the Hanoverians and he had been received everywhere with great acclaim; with his departure and the return to normal life, everyone including the Duke and Duchess resumed their customary and rather mundane existence. Yet the visit of George IV did have the effect of renewing family ties and over the next decade the Duke and Duchess made several trips to England. None of the sojourns were lengthy and on every occasion the Duchess always dreaded the prospect of crossing the Channel.

The death of George IV brought some changes for the Duke of Cambridge and his family. Firstly, in order to ensure that Prince George, now aged eleven, should have an English education he was sent to live at Windsor with King William IV. This was the reversal of the idea that had motivated George III to despatch his sons to Hanover. About the same time Count Münster retired and the Duke of Cambridge was officially named viceroy with much increased authority and was, until 1837, now the effective ruler of Hanover. Indeed, as recognition of the change in status the Duke was treated by the other German dynasties as if he were actually a reigning sovereign and he met them in equal terms and not merely as a sort of surrogate for his brother, King William IV.

In the spring of 1833 it was announced that the viceroy's wife was again expecting a child. Everyone was much surprised and this seems to have included the Duke and Duchess themselves since their last infant had been born more than a decade earlier. There was considerable concern for her health as she was now thirty-five and she was woefully alarmed herself about her situation. This agitation of mind affected her husband and he became quite unwell fussing himself into a nervous state and only recovered after the infant's birth on 27th November. His sister, writing a month later, informed her friend Miss Swinburne, 'Adolphus is a great deal better.'

As was customary in royal circles, the baby princess was given a string of names – *Mary* after her aunt, the Duchess of Gloucester and favourite sister of the Duke of Cambridge,

who doted on 'dearest Minny', *Adelaide* after her aunt who
was the consort of King William IV, *Wilhelmina* in honour of
the latter and *Elizabeth* after a third aunt, the Landgravine of
Hesse-Homburg and a sister of her father. Within the family,
however, she was to be known either as Mary or Mary
Adelaide. Some six weeks after her birth the formal christening ceremony took place in Hanover. Of her several
godparents, only her elderly aunt, the Landgravine Princess
Elizabeth was present but there were numerous guests and
officials in attendance all in court dress in honour of the
occasion. The baby was swathed in a long robe '*à drap d'ar-
gent* all tied with pink bows, and an enormous long train of
the same all trimmed with fine Brussels lace'. The infant
princess generally behaved well but she gave a loud cry when
the cold water from the font was placed on her head. Her
brother George, who had come to Hanover for the occasion,
described the event very succinctly: 'Yesterday evening the
christening of Mary took place. A most solemn and beautiful
ceremony and the service was well performed by Mr Ward...
I signed my name as a witness.' To a fourteen-year old
brother, a christening was not particularly exciting but it did
provide him with the reason to visit his parents, whom he saw
only infrequently. The christening also enabled the Hanoverians to show their loyalty to the reigning family and everywhere the Duke and his family went, they were greeted with
cheers and acclaim. A fortnight after the christening the viceroy gave a ball in honour of his daughter's birth. Of this event
her brother George observed, 'The Hanoverians are great
eaters of suppers.' Evidently there was little else that was
noteworthy.

Because her brother and sister were considerably older
than herself, Princess Mary Adelaide was something of a
novelty. The entire family doted on her and rather tended to
spoil her. Moreover, the Duchess was a somewhat nervous
and fussy mother and consequently she was overly concerned
about the child. Every minor ailment was a major illness,
every cry the shriek of pain – teething, for example, was a

traumatic crisis for the mother – and there tended to be excessive cosseting. Fortunately Princess Mary Adelaide was a cheerful and healthy baby on the whole and she flourished with all of the tender, loving care she received.

The viceregal establishment was one of some grandeur; the Duke of Cambridge had a good income of £27,000. He was provided with an official residence in Hanover and various country retreats all of which allowed for considerable court life. For some half dozen years the Cambridges acted as if they were truly the rulers of Hanover and kept up the standards required of a royal establishment. There were the usual *Kammerherren* and *Hochdamen*, secretaries and chaplains, governesses and nurses, as well as a large domestic staff. Visits from royal relations were events of note and when the Duke of Cumberland, the heir to the kingdom, arrived, there was a very real stir. Even the little princess noted that something unusual was afoot and enquired somewhat plaintively, 'Who are these strangers?' because the attention given to them meant that she was no longer at the centre of the stage.

Despite her known antipathy to a Channel crossing the Duchess of Cambridge was determined to present her youngest child to King William and Queen Adelaide. In the summer of 1836 the entire family met at Windsor and this provided the only occasion for the old king to meet his niece and infant god-daughter. Before a year was out, he was dead and the Cambridges were no longer resident in Hanover.

On 20th June 1837 William IV died and his niece became Queen; the Duke of Cambridge now ceased to act as viceroy because his brother Ernest had succeeded to the Hanoverian throne as a result of the application of the Salic Law. As the youthful Prince George was to note in his diary, 'My uncle, the Duke of Cumberland, has now become King of that Country [Hanover], and my cousin Princess Victoria is Queen of England.... Our position in the world is entirely changed.' The Duke of Cambridge, who had consorted with sovereigns as an equal, was now only the youngest brother of the King of Hanover and the uncle of the Queen of England.

The Leinstrasse in Hanover, to the right is the Altes Palace. The Cambridges lived in these royal residences from 1819 to 1837 while the Duke was Viceroy.
(After a painting by Kretschmer)

Princess Mary aged about four or five years. This romantic portrait was painted by Ziegler and is typical of the period.
(From Kinloch Cooke — courtesy John Murray)

H.R.H. Prince Ernest, Duke of Cumberland and later King of Hanover. He was extremely unpopular in England but well liked in Germany. When he succeeded to the throne in 1837 he revoked the liberal constitution that had been in effect while his brother, the Duke of Cambridge, was Viceroy.
(A painting by Kruger from a copy in a private collection)

Essentially, they were now like many other minor royal personages. They were really part of the court furniture.

The Duke did not long remain in Hanover; his brother's arrival was expected almost immediately and he and his family were soon packed and ready to return to England. The leave-taking was an emotional one and the Duke's farewell address indicated his sentiments. He referred to the people of Hanover as 'beloved inhabitants', he reminded them of his long association with the country and how 'many happy hours' he and his family had with 'those whom... [he] loved and esteemed'. However, it was now time to say goodbye. His sojourn in Germany was over and he concluded his remarks, 'Dearly beloved people of this Kingdom, I wish you all an affectionate adieu and leave you in the hope that you also will hereafter think with affection of me.' Very well indeed might they regret his departure for King Ernest immediately tore up the liberal constitution of 1831 and for the rest of his long reign proceeded to rule his kingdom as an absolute monarch.

It cannot have been particularly easy for the Cambridges to slip back into a rather mundane life in England. The Duke had not really lived in his own country since 1813 and the Duchess had never resided in Britain having previously only made fleeting visits. While their position in society was secure enough, as far as a public life was concerned they were virtually to be without occupation. The Duke was sixty-three, in appearance somewhat odd with a blond wig which he wore from time to time, and a sort of beard called a Newport fringe. He was rather eccentric and was inclined to chatter away in a loud voice at inappropriate moments. His wife, whose youthful slim figure had been so admired on her marriage, was now rather stout. Her English was heavily interlaced with German phrases and she had a thick accent which made conversation with strangers far from easy. Sensibly the royal couple recognized the new state of affairs and accepted their changed situation for neither had any desire to try and outshine their niece who was also their Queen.

Nevertheless, they and their children did not intend to abandon society and disappear from public view. They had a London house in Piccadilly – now the Naval and Military Club – and a rural retreat at Kew. Cambridge Cottage, as this rustic residence was called, had been the Duke's home as a boy and again from 1803 to 1813. He had occupied it but rarely during the time he had been viceroy and only then for a few days on his visits to England. Cambridge Cottage was not suitable as a family home but with additions and improvements it could be more than adequate. It was never particularly large being essentially 'a gentleman's residence' and of no particular architectural style or merit. However, it was agreeable and attractive, comfortable and relatively inexpensive to maintain. Moreover, the life at Kew was such that there was no need for a large establishment; the Duke had two equerries, one English and one Hanoverian, a secretary, as well as a chaplain – the latter was the Reverend Mr Ward who had been with the ducal couple in Hanover and who had baptized Princess Mary Adelaide; the Duchess had the usual ladies in waiting and like her husband, one from Germany and one from England. There was the usual domestic staff – something in the order of twenty – to ensure that the residents of Cambridge Cottage were suitably catered to; the whole establishment was very well managed, a great contrast to the muddle that existed at Windsor until Prince Albert reorganized the domestic side of the Queen's household.

The people in Kew were much pleased that the Cambridges had decided to be their neighbours. The Duke and Duchess were not excessively grand and they had a nice affability which allowed them to live on easy terms with the local population and to be more part of society in general than Queen Victoria and her Consort ever managed to do. The Cambridges really personified an older tradition in which royalty were able to select their friends and acquaintances in the widest possible sense rather than confining them almost exclusively to other royal personages as became the custom in the nineteenth century. Indeed, there was an unfortunate tendency that was to develop in the course of the nineteenth century when members of reigning families became excessively clannish; thereby, they lost contact with the real world and lived in an overly protected situation. This was to mean that many princes and princesses had too little understanding of the forces that directed events or of the attitudes of the population as a whole. Indeed, the Cambridges were amazingly aware of popular sentiment and received the approbation of the public largely because they were not socially invisible and because they were seen to be part of the national life.

Princess Mary Adelaide was not quite four years old when her parents and sister made their home in Kew. She was an attractive little girl with bright blue eyes – a Hanoverian family trait – a pink and white complexion and long golden hair. However, it was not already noted by observers that she was quite a large child but for the moment nobody seems to have thought this a difficulty. It was only as she became older that her size and weight was to become excessive. Because she was very much younger than her sister she was really almost like an only child. Her elderly father doted on this 'baby' and indulged her whims. For company to amuse her, the Duke and Duchess called upon the children of the local gentry who were frequently invited to Cambridge Cottage.

When Princess Mary Adelaide was seven, Miss Draper was appointed to be her governess. A proper school-room was set up and lessons began on a regular basis. She was taught the usual subjects that were thought to be suitable for a young lady; in addition to reading, writing and arithmetic, there was geography, music, sketching and also history. Like most members of the royal family she was to become interested in history and especially that of her own family. Not all her ancestors won her approbation and on one occasion she observed tartly 'Can it be possible that when I go to heaven I shall meet that murderer Henry VIII? Never! I can't believe it – such a bad character.'

Upon her accession Queen Victoria had written to the

Duke of Cambridge, 'I trust you will always find me an affectionate niece to an uncle who has always been kind to me. I rejoice to see you soon, as also, I hope, my Aunt and dear cousins. Pray dear Uncle, give them my best love.' Yet she was not overly intimate with his family. They made the occasional visits to see her and she was always pleased enough to receive them but her life and their own were very different. The 'old royal family' all hoped that perhaps Prince George and Queen Victoria might marry; certainly King William IV had such a possibility in mind when he brought his nephew to England to ensure that the young man have a proper education and outlook. Moreover, King William was suspicious of the intentions of the Duchess of Kent and her brother, King Leopold of Belgium, for he was apprehensive that they would try to enlarge their influence by promoting a marriage with a Saxe-Coburg.

The idea of an alliance between Prince George of Cambridge and his cousin was not one that appealed to either of them. Throughout their lives they were to be on excellent terms but only as cousins. Initially, the young Queen was in no great haste to marry but she knew that it was inevitable; she had great confidence in her uncle Leopold and she was willing to accept advice from him on the subject. He had a ready candidate, as King William IV suspected, namely his nephew Prince Albert the younger son of the reigning Duke of Saxe-Coburg. Prince Albert's good looks and personal charm appealed to Queen Victoria and they became engaged. Instead of heartfelt congratulations coming from the family a series of disagreements followed mainly over the question of precedence of the prospective bridegroom. By English custom the uncles of the sovereign took precedence over the husband of the sovereign and since the question of precedence was one which exercised the minds of all royal personages it was a matter which they felt touched them deeply. For example, mediatized princes and their families who were called 'Serene Highness' were less prestigious than sovereign princes and their families who were called 'Highness'. Moreover, some

Princess Mary aged six. This is an engraving of a painting by Landseer which bore the title 'On Trust'.

princes and princesses went into 'the closet' with reigning princes while others did not. To the modern mind this is all very insignificant but to people like the Dukes of Cambridge and Sussex in England and to their brother in Germany the matter was of the highest importance. What was a mere Prince of Saxe-Coburg in comparison with a Prince of Great Britain?

Much to the fury of Queen Victoria the Duke of Cambridge refused to allow Prince Albert to be next in rank to his wife. The Duke of Sussex was more amenable and was rewarded ultimately by having his 'wife' created Duchess of Inverness. The Duke of Cambridge was probably abetted by his brother, King Ernest of Hanover, who had his own reasons for wishing to annoy his niece. He claimed she was keeping certain family jewels which were properly his. The King of Hanover put his views very sharply and this stiffened the opposition of the Duke of Cambridge.

The precedence question completely divided the whole family. In a search for a solution they appealed to the Duke of Wellington whose position in society was unassailable and for whom everyone had respect. Wellington when he was informed officially on the matter was very sharp and abrupt in his response. He informed the Duke of Cambridge and his family, and indirectly the King of Hanover, that the Queen had the right to give anyone she liked precedence over her relations and that they would be wise and sensible to accept her wishes. The 'old royal family' were stunned by this attitude for they had assumed that he would be on their side. After considerable fussing and with rather bad grace the Duke of Cambridge acquiesced in his niece's wishes. Only Queen Adelaide, King William IV's widow, had kept her sanity in the matter and had tried to mollify and assuage the feelings of her relations on both sides. The affair left scars and Queen Victoria, thereafter, was never inclined to treat 'the old royal family' with as much concern and regard as in the past. However, they were all invited to her wedding and included in the party was her youngest cousin, Princess Mary Adelaide. The little girl was part of the official procession walking hand in hand with her mother; apparently her appearance provoked a number of approving comments about her exemplary behaviour and her looks but also it was now noted that she was somewhat large for her age.

In the summer following the Queen's wedding, the Duchess of Cambridge and her daughters went to the continent for an extended tour. They visited Rome, where they were indefatigable in observing all the major sights and assiduously visiting churches and galleries. Princess Mary was frequently left outside because her mother feared she might catch some disease as the interiors of the buildings were very damp. Later she remarked 'I was always left ... under the charge of an attendant, whose one idea of amusing me was to run me up and down ... the whole time.' As was their family custom they passed part of the summer at Rumpenheim and here they ended their lengthy holiday.

Once the family were back in Kew the Duchess decided to make some changes with respect to her younger daughter's education. It seemed sensible to employ a more professional preceptress and Sophia Howard was chosen to take charge. The new governess did not find it an easy task to induce her pupil to take a serious interest in her school work. Miss Howard soon discovered that her charge was excitable, emotional and impulsive as well as being very self-willed and rather inclined to obstinacy. This last characteristic was very much a family failing. Over time Sophia Howard won the confidence of her pupil and was able to control the child's behaviour but she was only successful by being exceedingly tactful as well as being firm. It is never easy to cope with royal personages. At times they regard those around them as friends and on other occasions they become very haughty and distant. However, in her efforts to guide and instruct the princess the governess was given unqualified support by her parents for they recognized that decisions concerning their daughter were made for her benefit even if they found that Sophia Howard's views were not always designed for their convenience. They were sensible enough to recognize that, such was Princess Mary Adelaide's character, had they interfered the child would have taken advantage of the situation and played one authority against another with no good in the long term for anyone. In due course Miss Howard was to become a great friend of her pupil but the first year cannot have been easy. Moreover, the governess had to adjust herself to a different world as well since she was in attendance constantly whether it was at Kew, Rumpenheim or Windsor.

In 'the great game', that is, the royal marriage stakes, the elder daughter of the Cambridges was a qualified player. The managing royal mammas and aunts as they sat with their ladies had contemplated and considered her prospects. All were delighted when she became engaged to her cousin Frederick the heir to the grand Duchy of Mecklenburg-Strelitz. Princess Augusta's position was now secure; ultimately she would be the consort of a reigning prince. Of course Strelitz was not the centre of the universe – indeed, it was reckoned to be one of the most conservative and traditional of the small German courts – but it was better to be the centre of attention if only in a small world than a mere dependant in a major kingdom. The marriage of the cousins took place on 28th June 1843; it was the occasion for a gathering of the 'royal mob' with Queen Victoria and Prince Albert having pride of place after the parents of the bride and groom. The Houses of Hanover and Saxe-Coburg were temporarily one in indicating that not every day did a Princess of Great Britain marry a German princeling. The principals in the cast were supported by numerous aunts, uncles and cousins all of whom added to the scene. Since the Cambridge family were popular with British society, the country showed its approbation and the young couple were showered with gifts.

The departure of Princess Augusta left a considerable gap at Kew. The Duchess who had relied on her elder daughter for companionship was forced to fall back on others. Princess Mary Adelaide was only ten. She had adored her sister and was constantly observing 'I wonder if I shall be as clever' and

'Augusta is so handsome'. She feared she would not really be capable of filling the gap. It was only when she grew older that she was able to take her sister's place. To resolve the situation temporarily the Duchess decided to go to Rumpenheim in Hesse to be with her relations.

Schloss Rumpenheim was the gathering place of the descendents of Landgraf Frederick of Hesse, the property having belonged to his mother, a daughter of George II of England. She had retired to live on the estate when her husband had become a Roman Catholic. Rumpenheim was 'built quite in the style of an old country house'. It was situated near the River Main with gardens and parks sloping towards the river. The house itself was a three-sided building painted white; the central block was higher than the two wings and the latter consisted of suites of rooms. The Schloss was furnished rather simply and in a style that was thought modern a century earlier but by the 1840s it was rather old-fashioned. There was nothing grand about Rumpenheim; indeed Blenheim or Chatsworth were veritable palaces by comparison.

The six children of Landgraf Frederick owned the schloss jointly but only two of the princes, George and Frederick, resided there permanently. For the remainder it was a large holiday house. The guests took over sets of rooms – in the height of the season they were very crowded and often the young were stuffed into the attics – and brought their own staff; ladies-in-waiting, gentlemen in attendance and the like were ubiquitous. While they were able to live independently they took a number of meals in common and always met for dinner. Rumpenheim was a great place for gossip and matchmaking. Queen Victoria regarded the whole establishment with much suspicion, she knew that it was the centre of hostility to Prussian ambitions and she and Prince Albert believed the *Kleinstadtismus* so ardently supported by the Hessian family was contrary to the welfare of Germany and to any prospect of national unity. Moreover, Queen Victoria actively disliked many of the Hessian princes and princesses; she held that some of the women were 'low', that is, without

H.R.H. Augusta, Princess of Great Britain and Grand Duchess of Mecklenburg-Strelitz (b. 1822 — d. 1916) at the time of her marriage. A typical romantic portrait of the period.
(Collection Staatsarchiv Schwerin)

34

H.R.H. Frederick William, Grand Duke of Mecklenburg-Strelitz (b. 1819 — d. 1904) at the time of his marriage to Princess Augusta. He was a charming young man, well liked by the Cambridge family.
(Collection Staatsarchiv Schwerin)

good moral character, or that they were frivolous and un-
steady. There was really no truth to Queen Victoria's moral
strictures on Rumpenheim, it was simply a matter of pre-
judice. There is little doubt that she was also slightly jealous of
the good times that everyone seemed to have and consequently their pleasures and enjoyment took on a darker hue.

Life at Rumpenheim was not particularly exciting, it was
very much in the tradition of Marie Antoinette playing the
milkmaid at the Trianon. Princess Mary Adelaide was to
write 'On Sunday, it being a beautiful day, we walked to a
wood at some little distance and cooked ourselves a rural
luncheon and had all kinds of fun; indeed, we are such a party
that we amuse ourselves constantly in this kind of rural way,
for I think less the numbers less the fun'. To confirm this view
of the simple life, Lady Geraldine Somerset who was a member of the Duchess of Cambridge's household some years later
noted on another day 'We walked about... had a very good
rural luncheon after which they [the royals] all got very wild,
poking potatoes and squashed grapes down each other's necks
and into each other's pockets.' One can better understand the
amusement Albert Edward the Prince of Wales was to get
from squirting soda-water on his friends and putting ices
down their necks; it was evidently all part of the attempt to
live the way they imagined ordinary people did and to allow
themselves free rein when not on display.

Getting to Rumpenheim from England was somewhat
complicated. For one thing the Cambridges made quite a
party – there was the Duke and Duchess, Princess Mary
Adelaide, a lady-in-waiting and a gentleman, Miss Howard,
and the chaplain, as well as valets, maids, coachmen, grooms
and the like. Since the Duchess had such a horror of the
Channel crossing every effort had to be made that she should
not suffer more than was necessary. Mountains of luggage
had to be loaded on to the packet because one had to have an
extensive wardrobe. Although technically *en villageature*, the
denizens of Rumpenheim dressed for dinner each evening.
Princess Mary Adelaide took her lesson books – she was not

permitted to be totally idle – as well as sketching paper and her music so that she might have 'some duets to play with... [the] cousins'.

Three days after they departed from Kew they arrived at Rumpenheim where they remained for two months. The Duke of Cambridge did not stay the whole time but made forays to visit friends and relatives. Apparently he found it all a bit stultifying and tedious. The Duchess and her daughter were joined by Princess Augusta and her husband so there was a nice reunion. At the end of October the Cambridges made ready to move on to visit Hanover and Saxony and they required a total of eight carriages to convey them and their household and their luggage on the first part of the journey.

For the Cambridges their first visit to Hanover since 1837, as guests of King Ernest, provided them with the opportunity to see old friends. They had been very discreet and had kept their distance when they had left the country but now enough time had elapsed and their return would not cause any jealousy. For Princess Mary, the holiday in Hanover meant that she became acquainted with her cousins; she was much charmed by Prince George and felt very sorry for him as 'his blindness... [was] a great affliction'.

They all moved on from Hanover to Saxony and took up residence in Dresden. It was here that Princess Mary Adelaide celebrated her tenth birthday; the King and Queen gave a party in honour of the occasion and she was the recipient of many presents from the family and the court. The Christmas celebrations a month later were equally gay and once again she received many gifts. In a letter to Eleanor Draper, her former governess, Princess Mary Adelaide said that she had been given 'a handsome china soup-basin, saucer and ladle... a complete band of monkeys in china... a doll... [and] an antique necklace and earrings'. After the festivities of Twelfth Night the Cambridges made ready to return to Kew travelling first to Frankfurt and from there to Calais. For once the Channel was very smooth and the crossing took less than two hours; even the Duchess had no signs of seasickness.

Once back in Cambridge Cottage, the princess and her governess resumed their usual routine; there were lessons and walks during the week, scriptures to be learned for church on Sunday. There were occasional diversions: visits to Windsor to see the Queen and the baby Princess Victoria, luncheons and teas with the elderly aunts, calls to be made on the local gentry. But generally life was unexciting. This was to be the basic pattern of Princess Mary Adelaide's existence for the next few years. To be sure, there were some indications that the little girl was now entering into adult society. She attended a fancy dress ball at Windsor but was only a spectator – a sign to all that the princess was not yet 'out' – and she went to the theatre to see the famous dancers, Taglioni, Grisi, Cherito and Grahn in *Les Sylphides*, a ballet specially choreographed for them when they were all *ballerinas assolutas* and so arranged that none could claim pride of place.

Certain traits of character were now fixed; she liked collecting – she had a great enthusiasm for her possessions and her numerous dolls she kept even after she was married – she was humane and good-willed, a perpetual optimist, and she was pious. These are positive aspects of her personality, the more negative elements were her unpunctuality, which irritated people, her stubbornness which resulted in her being aggrieved and often petulant, and her generosity which was almost thoughtless and often excessive thereby inconveniencing not only her immediate family but others as well. Despite an easy manner she expected the deference due to her rank and once said to a young friend 'I am Princess Mary Adelaide of Great Britain and Ireland' making it very clear that she recognized that her royal rank set her apart from her acquaintances.

In 1845 after the usual sojourn at Rumpenheim the family went on to Strelitz for the autumn, remaining until after Christmas. Strelitz was generally regarded as being very provincial but the Cambridges enjoyed the simple life, accepted the limitations of the society and were seemingly totally content. It was very much a family circle; the Duchess of Cambridge was not only sister to the reigning Grand Duchess

A view of the residence of the Grand Duke of Mecklenburg-Strelitz. The Cambridge family spent much time here over the years. Life in the Schloss was very formal — a real contrast to the casual life at Rumpenheim.

but mother-in-law to the heir who was her nephew. Moreover, they seemed able to continue living much as they did at Rumpenheim with their own apartments and their own attendants. Nevertheless there was a formality at Strelitz which did not prevail either at Kew or Rumpenheim. This less easy regime meant that special occasions such as wedding anniversaries and birthdays were times requiring notice. Consequently when Princess Mary Adelaide's twelfth birthday occurred, her uncle, the Grand Duke, took due notice of the event and arranged a court ball for her. The highlight of the evening apparently came when the Princess and her party, wearing Greek costumes, danced a polka. She naïvely records, 'It was much applauded.' Simple folk were easily gratified. While royal personages were required to maintain the ceremony due to their rank in public, within their own circle they were almost bourgeois. The children made simple presents for their relations: they knotted bags, crocheted mittens, did Berlin work, painted pictures and the like. In return their family were often very generous giving them things such as bracelets made of hair and ornamented with gold clasps, bronze statuettes of legendary heros, and cheerful prints of suitable and jolly subjects. There are few references to receiving books except for those illustrated albums which lay on tables in the drawing rooms and which were perused each evening to idle away some of the time that was not passed in family games.

At the grand-ducal Schloss in Neu Strelitz Christmas festivities were very traditional. Everyone had their own table upon which was placed a small tree and there were flowers and swags as decoration. On each table were the presents and also baskets of sweets and other favours which were distributed to members of the household. The trees were decorated with candles and in the course of the evening they were all set alight – a very real fire hazard but one that was accepted – to give the room a magical appearance.

Princess Mary Adelaide and her parents returned to England in January 1846. The journey back was most uncomfortable, travelling was difficult and the Channel crossing took three and a half hours during which time the Duchess as usual was very seasick. When they got home they found that there had been a fire at Cambridge Cottage but this was ultimately to result in an improvement. The rooms most severely damaged had formerly been occupied by servants, they were now thrown into one to provide a sitting room for the Princess Augusta when she came to stay and could be used by the household on other occasions.

At Cambridge Cottage lessons were begun once more. Miss Howard continued her work as governess. Italian was added, a new subject of study, but otherwise things were unchanged. Life was not all drudgery and Princess Mary had breaks from the usual pattern of her quiet life. The christening of Princess Helena at Windsor was a great affair, and Princess Mary felt very grown up being allowed to attend the banquet given by the Queen. She had much pleasure in sitting next to the Duke of Wellington, with whom she felt very much at ease, but he was known to be pleasant to the young. In the late autumn she went to the opera, made frequent visits to the aunts and there were a number of excursions to London; the highlight was a family gathering at Windsor to celebrate the new year. Princess Mary, who doted on her young cousins, described them: 'The Princess Royal is my pet, because she is remarkably clever. The Prince of Wales is a very pretty boy, but he does not talk as much as his sister. Little Alfred, the fourth child, is a beautiful fatty, with lovely hair. Alice is rather older than him [*sic*], she is very modest and quiet, but very good natured. Helena, the baby, is a very fine child, and very healthy.'

Since Princess Mary was now almost fourteen her mother decided that her daughter no longer needed a governess and early in February Miss Howard departed. Lessons were now conducted differently with the Baroness Hammerstein, the Duchess of Cambridge's lady-in-waiting, initially in charge. Later Baroness Böse was to assume the position of *grande-gouvernante*, a post she held for a year, but the arrangement

H.R.H. Prince George, Duke of Cambridge as a young
man in a painting by Winterhalter. This portrait like
others by the same artist was very flattering to the sitter.
(From a photograph in a private collection of an original
painting in the Royal Collection)

Louisa Fairbrother, 'Mrs Fitzgeorge', the so-called 'wife'
of H.R.H. Prince George, Duke of Cambridge. The
marriage was never recognised legally and Mrs
Fitzgeorge was never received by the Royal family. The
couple had three sons whose existence was only
marginally noticed by their relations.
(After a painting by Joy — courtesy Longman Group)

was not satisfactory and thereafter the Duchess herself over-saw the activities of the various teachers whom she employed. Princess Mary very much missed the companionship of Miss Howard who had been with her for seven years. A year after she left the royal household the former governess married a Doctor Laumann who kept a school; Dr Laumann had the disadvantage of being a widower with six children but these defects were balanced by the fact that he was comfortably off so 'dear Howard' was suitably provided for.

Early in 1847 the entire Cambridge family were stunned to learn that Prince George was 'married'. He had lived for some time with Louisa Fairbrother and they had two children, George and Adolphus, born in 1843 and 1846 respectively. A third son, Augustus, was to be born in the summer of 1847. Prince George had long maintained that arranged marriages were generally unsuccessful and frequently very unhappy. He had found no princesses that had attracted his attention and as he was well removed from the succession he could please himself. He knew of the provision of the Royal Marriages Act which required the sovereign's consent for the legality of a marriage of a prince or princess. He was well aware that his uncle the Duke of Sussex had violated the law on two occasions and that his wives were never given royal rank. He knew too that under British law the idea of a morganatic marriage did not exist. Nevertheless, he was determined to act according to his own wishes. A form of marriage occurred on the eighth of January. He always regarded himself as Louisa Fairbrother's husband in the sight of God if not under the law, declining ever to consider any change in his domestic situation. His wife took the name of Mrs Fitzgeorge and this was the surname of their sons.

Queen Victoria never recognized her cousin's situation; for her officially, at least, he remained unmarried. Mrs Fitzgeorge's position was purely a private one, she was never given a title as was Lady Cecilia Underwood, the wife of the Duke of Sussex. Nor was she ever received by the Queen and it is questionable whether they ever met. The sons were never accepted as being part of the family by Queen Victoria although she knew about them and was to see them when one or another acted either as their father's A.D.C. or secretary.

Once the initial consternation of the family was over, each member of Prince George's family decided on their own form of acceptance. Apparently a year after the marriage the Duke of Cambridge saw Louisa Fitzgeorge on Constitution Hill and, as she said, 'He kissed his hand to me for no person was near'. The Duchess never acknowledged her so-called daughter–in–law although she was to leave the three Fitzgeorge boys the sum of £5,000 each in her will. Neither Princess Augusta nor Princess Mary ever received their so-called 'sister–in–law' and indeed once while driving in the Park when the Princess Mary's lady-in-waiting pointed out Louisa Fitzgeorge, the former was very excited, asked to have her identified: 'Where is she? I have never yet seen her'. Prince George led two lives, one cozy and domestic, the other royal and public.

This family crisis had no effect on Princess Mary. She continued her lessons under Baroness Hammerstein's supervision and had her portrait painted by Winterhalter at Windsor, saying of the picture, 'It is considered an excellent likeness'. As this was 'the season' the Cambridges had migrated from Kew to London. This move was not entirely to the princess's liking. For her the house in the country was ever 'dear sweet charming Kew.... To exchange the green lawns and gardens of *dear old Kew* for that *horrid* London with all its smoke and dirt is too shocking to think of.' It made the occasional rural excursion more delightful: 'We have twice been to Kew... how beautiful it was.' Town life had its compensations however, there was a fête for children, Queen Victoria attended with her 'three dear little children who all concerned themselves very much'. The entertainment consisted of a play called *Gamin de Paris*, a concert of two harps and a violin played by children, a dance by a ballerina and 'a child [who] walked upon a globe... stood upon it while it went backwards and forwards, and danced upon it' – a very 'wonderful sight'. There were tumblers, Ethiopian singers in blackface and a floral dance.

Despite her enjoyment of the pleasures of society, Princess Mary Adelaide had always shown a real interest and concern for religion. She was a devout Anglican, noting in a letter to a friend a few years later, 'My heart is truly Protestant.' The Reverend Mr Ward and his successor the Reverend Mr Harrison who taught her scripture had a very real influence on her, they curbed her impulsiveness and imbued in her a sense of seriousness of purpose – a concern in particular for those less fortunate than herself, which later was to manifest itself in her numerous charitable activities. She even composed a special prayer for herself. It was evident that even she recognized her impulsiveness and her other character defects.

Almighty Father, I pray Thee to look down on Thy erring child, and teach me to subdue my proud rebellious nature. Grant that I may be humble and submissive to my dear parents and to all that are given authority over me; and whenever I may offend Thee by pride, self-will, or disobedience, I beseech Thee to make me sincerely penitent and sorry for my transgressions, and send me Thy grace, that I may endeavour to amend my conduct for the time to come, and walk in Thy blessed ways, through Jesus Christ our Lord. Amen.

As usual the family went to Rumpenheim in the summer of 1847. Princess Mary, although officially having a holiday, continued her lessons. Her day was fully occupied and marked out with almost Prussian military precision. She rose at half-past-six, dressed and walked in the garden; at nine she and Baroness Hammerstein took breakfast together; at ten Pastor Ulrich came for two hours – he taught various subjects such as history and geography; at noon she wrote her daily journal – it appears that the keeping of a diary was almost a sacred obligation for young princesses; shortly before one she took a light luncheon and then practised her music for an

H.R.H. Princess Thyra of Denmark, who married George, Prince of Hanover and Duke of Cumberland. Like her sisters, she was a great friend of Princess Mary and shared many of her political attitudes.
(From the collection of H.M. The Queen of Denmark, Royal Library, Copenhagen)

hour; twice a week a music mistress arrived to give further instruction; at two there was another short walk followed by more lessons, the last rather brief, then dinner in full dress at four o'clock – the meal lasted two hours; from six to seven in the evening, reading aloud to the older generation in French or English – a good many of the elderly took the opportunity to doze off after a heavy meal; from seven to eight she was free to be as idle as she liked; at eight another collation when tea was served and at nine she retired. Of course there were breaks in the routine, when no work was required: birthdays, name days and the like were times of celebration. Then, too, there were expeditions to neighbouring villages and towns or for more extensive rural walks, the latter providing opportunities for sketching. It cannot be said that her life was exciting but it seems that she found it agreeable enough because her parents were determined to ensure that her head was not turned by flattery or worldliness. Political events did not seem to touch her.

This was all to change in 1848. The Cambridges being so closely related to the Danish Royal Family were deeply concerned with the outbreak of revolution in Schleswig-Holstein. Princess Mary was a strong partisan of the Danes and opposed the pretensions of the Germanic Confederation which insisted the Duchies remain German states at all costs. The problem of Schleswig and Holstein was not to be resolved until 1852 – they remained part of the Confederation – but even then as events turned out the solution was only temporary. While the Schleswig-Holstein question interested the family they were not as directly concerned as they were to be over other events in Germany and in particular in Strelitz.

Initially the revolutionary movement had little effect in Strelitz and indeed the local population seemingly were filled with pleasure when the Grand Duchess Augusta produced an heir. 'The people of Strelitz were so happy when they had a little *Erbprinz*' the princess wrote in a letter to Miss Draper, her former governess, and she continued, 'They fired the cannons and the bands of the *Burgergarde* began to play

before the Palace; they dined in the open air, and in the
evening they illuminated the whole town. My sister's picture
was hung out at every window surrounded with lights.'
However such loyal sentiment was to change. The establishment of the Frankfurt Parliament and with it the call for more
liberal government finally had its effect even in conservative
Strelitz, with the people demanding free elections and a
change of ministry. The Grand Duke refused these requests
with the result that there were riots and considerable damage
ensued. Soldiers were sent into the capital to restore order
which was done quickly. The Grand Duchess Augusta and
the little Prince Adolphus George Frederick Augustus Victor
Wellington had been hurried away from all danger. Some
concessions were made to the popular demands; universal
suffrage was granted and 'labourers' were actually elected to
the commission to write the new constitution. Princess Mary,
never one to mince words, laid the blame for all of the troubles
on Lord Palmerston, whom she accused of meddling and
interfering 'to the great detriment of the Monarchical government and to the advantage of the radical party'. She certainly
would have sympathized with the Prussians who said:

> If the devil had a son
> Surely he'd be Palmerston.

Indeed, throughout her whole life Princess Mary was to be
intensely politically conservative and to distrust liberals of any
kind.

The situation in Germany continued to be difficult. For
some months the German National Assembly, meeting in
Frankfurt, was wrestling with a new constitution with little
real success. Meanwhile the more conservative elements in
the various states were regaining their authority. Prussia,
which had been convulsed with revolution in the summer,
was symbolic. By November General Wrangel entered Berlin
with the army, the citizen guard was disbanded, Strelitz was
no longer in danger and the Grand Duchess Augusta and her

family were unlikely to be at risk. However, plans had been made for her to come to England if the situation warranted it.

While the Grand Ducal family from Strelitz were not forced to take refuge in England a number of people had to do so. Prince Metternich, the former all-powerful Austrian Chancellor, and his wife were in Brighton as were Princess Lieven and Guizot, the Chief Minister of Louis-Philippe. The latter, now in exile, was in residence at Claremont, a house lent by Queen Victoria as a residence for himself and his family. The Cambridges received many of these notables and Princess Mary was much impressed with Prince Metternich: 'It was very interesting... to see a man who for so many years has governed the Austrian Empire, and for whose cleverness and talents as a statesman all European countries have had the greatest respect.' She did not pause to consider, however, why he was now in exile. He and his wife were to take up residence in Kew and to become very friendly with the Cambridge family. Princess Lieven frightened the young girl somewhat but she was apparently gratified when the Russian princess paid her polite attention; Princess Lieven, whatever her opinion of royal personages, and frequently she regarded them with little respect, was always scrupulously careful in her relations with them and this instance was no exception.

Princess Mary was now in her sixteenth year. With the departure of Baroness Böse, the system of *grande-gouvernante* was given up. Her departure was not much regretted by her pupil. She wrote to Elinor Draper 'The Baroness Böse has left me for good... I will not say anything about her excepting she has returned to Germany and is looking out for a situation. I pity her extremely for she has not made herself friends.' The Princess even went so far as to indicate that her own lack of good manners and humour was entirely the result of the bad influence of the Baroness. Lessons of a sort were continued but they were in a more relaxed level and more and more time was spent in ladylike occupations fitting her position in society.

Despite the restoration of order in Strelitz, the political

H.R.H. Augusta, Grand Duchess of Mecklenburg-Strelitz, in her middle years. Note how very similar she is in appearance to her younger sister Princess Mary. Princess Augusta was always to feel nostalgia for England in 'exile' in Strelitz.
(Collection Staatsarchiv Schwerin)

H.R.H. Frederick William, Grand Duke of Mecklenburg-Strelitz and brother-in-law of Princess Mary. He was called Fritz by the family and was a great favourite with them all. In old age he went blind but he retained a very real sense of dignity to the end.
(Collection Staatsarchiv Schwerin)

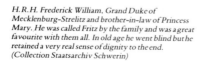

situation was still alarming and concern was felt by all at Cambridge Cottage for their relations. They knew that Fritz was very conservative and Princess Mary Adelaide felt that he was 'harassed by all of the sad events that occur in Germany' and not in any way sympathetic 'to the republican spirit' which was evident 'in all classes at present'. All at Cambridge Cottage were unhappy 'at the melancholy accounts we receive of the fearful state of the continent' with the prospect of further violence in Frankfurt and the very real fear that Rumpenheim itself would be the object of an attack. The Landgraf Frederick, her uncle, had removed himself to Cassel 'for to be in the *voisinage* of Frankfurt at such a moment is anything but agreeable'.

If news from the continent reported potential revolution and violence, life in England continued to be in the whole serene. The attempted assassination of Queen Victoria in late May 1849 upset everyone because it might seem to those outside the country that Britain was in a dangerously revolutionary situation which was not the case. The Chartists had failed to bring about change and the population on the whole were generally satisfied with the state of society. Indeed, there was a certain national smugness when the average Englishman compared his country to 'abroad'. Princess Mary's only concern was that Lord Palmerston's activities should be curtailed for she was convinced almost daily that he was bent in destroying the whole social order. As she said, 'These democratic principles will one day bring us to the scaffold.'

If political events conspired against the annual 'royal mob' gathering at Rumpenheim as it was to do in 1849, one of the principal activities of those who generally gathered there did not cease. Royal matchmaking did not seem to be in any way curtailed. Princess Mary's situation was already one of interest and various prospects for a husband were envisaged. One family who eyed an English matrimonial alliance was the House of Orange. King William II had been the rejected suitor of Princess Charlotte but his youngest son, Henry, decided to make a trip to England to investigate the possibility of an

English marriage. Prince Henry's sister-in-law Queen Sophie, the wife of King William III, was much in favour of the whole project. She herself approved of anything to prevent further Russian or Prussian influence at The Hague. In a letter to her friend, Lady Malet, she commented on the project, calling Prince Henry 'as silent slow and insignificant as ever' – hardly promising comment for a suitor – and adding somewhat dolefully, 'He will never have energy to propose'. When Prince Henry did return to the Netherlands in mid-June, she wrote again to her friend, 'Prince Henry is come back, over head and ears in love with Princess Mary of Cambridge… I should like the match. She is very clever, gay as a lark…' The courtship did not prosper and Prince Henry was to marry a Prussian princess four years later.

To compensate for being unable to travel to Germany, the Cambridge family – the Duke and Duchess, their daughters Mary and Augusta and the latter's baby Adolphus, whom she had newly brought to England – went to Wales. They stayed at *Plas Newydd* loaned to them by Lord Anglesey. The latter, a friend of the Duke of Wellington, was known as 'One-leg' having lost a limb at Waterloo. In his youth he had been a beau and had incurred the displeasure of his family and friends for running off with the wife of Wellington's brother and being cited as co-respondent in a divorce suit. He married the lady and the story was now virtually forgotten. Anglesey and his wife were very much respected by society, although there were some who never received them. But the Cambridges were very cordial.

The journey to Wales was a difficult and somewhat exhausting one; however, the advent of the railway had made it less arduous with the last part from Bangor across the suspension bridge by horse and carriage. *Plas Newydd* was an ideal holiday retreat, relatively remote and romantic in appearance. It was a sort of castle with gothic embellishments but it had been slightly modernized by its owner. It was not his principal residence – *Beaudeseú* served as that – and hence it had retained a sort of simplicity not unlike Rumpenheim. It allowed for similar activities with walks on the terrace, country expeditions to see the sights: the Menai Bridge, Caernarvon Castle and the Fall of the Swallow, and the local people with their folk costumes and their dialects not unlike the rural population in Germany.

'I am very much amused at being in Britain,' Princess Mary noted 'and not understanding the language of the people. Most of the poor people speak nothing but Welsh and do not understand English at all.' The quaint clothing of the women attracts her notice for they wore 'the peasant's dress and charming white caps with frills and black *wide awakes* and beaver hats, like the men, stuck on the top of their heads'. It was a world not far removed from that of the previous century and 'the Ladies of Llangollen'.

The sojourn in the country came to an end in the early autumn and the family returned to Kew. They were greeted by the news that Queen Adelaide was on her death bed. She had been ailing for some time and she expired on 2nd December. With her death and that of her sister-in-law Princess Sophia the year previously, the family circle of the older generation was much diminished. Only Princess Mary's aunts, the Duchesses of Kent and Gloucester, her uncle the Duke of Cumberland and her own parents still survived.

The Duke of Cambridge had also been ailing. He suffered acutely from gout and was frequently incapacitated. Much to his chagrin his activities were curtailed and his temper was not improved. He was now seventy-six and increasingly infirm. Nevertheless in the last winter of his life he continued to be as busy as in the past, appearing in public on occasion and participating in the family round. Indeed, so little concern was felt for him that his elder daughter and her son went back to Strelitz for it seemed as if the revolution in Germany was really at an end since the movement for some new confederation had collapsed. Schleswig-Holstein continued to be a problem with the outbreak of a new conflict between the Danes and the Duchies but the latter's troops were generally held in check by the soldiers of King Frederick VII. It seemed

53

as if the old order, more or less, was restored.

Quite suddenly in early summer the Duke of Cambridge was taken ill. His wife and younger daughter were constantly at his bedside and the Queen was assiduous in offering help and solace. The Victorians had a penchant for death-beds and funerals. Princess Mary's description of the melancholy events are very typical: 'The last day I never left him, for he liked to have me with him, when Mama was for a moment called away to fan him and bathe his temples with *eau de cologne* and then he would press my hand and whisper "charming," "dear"... [I have a] hallowed recollection of my dear Father as when I kissed his forehead for the last time a sweet and heavenly smile played on his lips, and but for their marble hue I could not have believed they were closed forever.' The Duke expired on 8th July and some six hours later his daughter Augusta arrived. 'Too late!' was her cry as she knelt beside his bed. The princess was to make a career of always arriving just too late for the last moments of her relations and it became a sort of joke that she would even fail to be present when her own time came.

The country was not plunged into mourning nor was there great grief when this the last but one of King George III's sons died. What the country regretted was the end of 'a prince who had inherited all the good looks of his family and none of its grossness, all its good taste and none of its prodigality, all its kindliness and few of its oddities, added to these a modesty and decency all his own'.

Following the funeral the family retired to Cambridge Cottage but shortly thereafter the widow, her daughters and grandson accepted the invitation of Lord Anglesey and went to *Plas Newydd* as they had the year before. The ladies and their household all swathed in yards of black repeated the journey to Bangor by train and then on to their residence by carriage. It was not the merry holiday that they had all experienced previously. After a couple of months' stay, they went back to Kew and to a melancholy homecoming.

The year's events concluded with the Princess being con-

H.M. King Christian IX of Denmark and Louise, his Queen, were part of the Rumpenheim circle and great friends of the Cambridge family. They met almost every year during the summer.
(From the collection of H.M. The Queen of Denmark, Royal Library, Copenhagen)

firmed in the Church at Kew shortly before Christmas. The whole family was present including the Queen and her husband and their older children and the service was conducted by the Bishop of London and the Archbishop of Canterbury. The Princess was deeply moved by the ceremony. All that was lacking was 'Dear Papa's blessing'. As a memento, however, she had been given a marble sculpture of her father's hand 'so very like and so well done'.

With the Duke's death a stage in the Princess's life came to an end. Her brother was now the Duke and he had inherited Cambridge House and Cambridge Cottage, although his mother and sisters continued to use the latter for a number of years. The Duchess took up residence in St James's Palace in rooms allocated to her by Queen Victoria and here she lived when she was in London. She was to spend more and more of her time in town and this was to mean that her younger daughter was, once the long mourning was complete, to be in the midst of society. Since Princess Mary was fourteen years younger than Queen Victoria (who was much occupied with her children and husband and was more often at Windsor than in London) and since she was unmarried, the result was that she, the princess, her brother and her mother were the only members of the royal family who were seen in general society. Moreover, while never forgetting their rank and position, the Cambridges presented another aspect of royalty and one that was less formal or serious than that of Queen Victoria and Prince Albert. In a sense it was in this period of her life that Princess Mary first came to be seen as a very popular figure by all classes in the kingdom.

CHAPTER TWO

'This Vast Undertaking'

Although the Duke of Cambridge had been dead for nearly six months, because of the conventions of the day his family continued to live in retirement. Christmas was kept quietly and the widowed Duchess and Princess Mary were joined at Kew by the Strelitz family – Augusta, Fritz and Adolphus – as well as by George who was given leave from his military duties in Ireland. However, the Duchess of Cambridge did not intend to allow her bereavement to blight the life of her younger daughter and once the new year started, the latter, now in her eighteenth year, began to go out into society in a limited manner. The first indication came in the spring when the princess, accompanied by a lady-in-waiting, was a guest of Lord Wilton and his wife. This resumption of social activity in a manner which the Cambridges had practised for some time past meant that Princess Mary was once again in the public eye. While the Duchess undertook no public duties, Princess Mary was allowed to be a member of the royal party at the opening ceremonies of the Crystal Palace. Accompanying her aunt the Duchess of Kent, Princess Mary arrived at the Crystal Palace just before the Queen, Prince Albert and their two elder children. All of the ladies were dressed as for a formal court, the men in uniform; the Queen wore a tiara and her orders, Prince Albert was in his uniform as a field marshal, the Prince of Wales was in highland costume, the Princess Royal was dressed in white satin with a wreath of primroses. The royal party with the Queen and Prince in the lead made their way to the central nave of the Palace. The national anthem was sung, the Prince formally read a report and the Queen replied. There was a brief prayer followed by the Hallelujah Chorus. At this juncture an elegant Chinese appeared from the midst of the invited guests and bowed low to the Queen and her family. He was commanded to join in the formal ceremonies. Everyone believed him to be a mandarin of high degree but in fact he was called He-Sing and his appearance was a sort of stunt. Once the procession had been formed the Queen made a short tour of inspection; all the while the organs were playing and at one stage a military band struck up the march from *Athalie* as the Queen passed in front of them. Everyone then returned to their original places and Lord Breadalbane was commanded to declare the Exhibition opened. This was followed by a flourish of trumpets; the Queen and other members of the royal family made their bows and departed. As the Queen said there were 'deafening cheers and waving of handkerchiefs' and 'Every face was bright and smiling'.

The princess's elderly aunt the Duchess of Gloucester wrote to Queen Victoria describing the day as her niece had reported it. 'Mary... came away in perfect *enchantement!*... And full of how pretty your dear little Victoria looked, and how nicely she was dressed and so grateful to your Mother for all her kindness to her.' After attending the Exhibition Princess Mary, her mother and her brother dined at Gloucester House and they drank the Queen's 'health at dinner and *congratulations* on the *complete success* of *Albert's plans* and *arrangements*'.

The Princess was almost as overwhelmed by it all as was Queen Victoria herself. She noted in a letter to a friend, 'The interior of the building was quite magnificent and a good proof of what England could do. High above all the nations of the world in her contributions she is far superior to them in many things, backward in none.' The Crystal Palace itself was 'the wonder of the world' and the 'truly loyal and enthusiastic reception given by John Bull to the Queen was very gratifying'. She goes on to say, '*We English* Royal family had a right to be proud of our country, and happy that foreigners should witness its loyalty. I would not have exchanged my title of Princess of England at that moment for that of Empress of the whole world.' Indeed, she never lost these sentiments and her disinclination to leave England was to prove a problem in the choice of a husband.

In order to have a more thorough tour of the building and its contents, Princess Mary made several visits to the Crystal Palace to view the exhibits as it had not been possible to look at everything on the opening day. Indeed, the Crystal Palace was for her as for everyone 'the only subject of conversation'. Aside from these excursions her daily routine was still that of the young lady who was 'not out'. She was not a schoolgirl – 'her hair had been put up' – but she had certain lessons and her education in an informal fashion was continued. Nevertheless, she was definitely released from the routine of the schoolroom and more and more she was a companion to her widowed mother.

As if to indicate that her period of formal mourning was over the Duchess once again decided upon an extended continental holiday. Once more she and her daughter passed a couple of months at Rumpenheim where they joined their Hessian relations. In August the Cambridges went on to Ischl which was the popular resort for the Austrian court and aristocracy. Here were to be found the Young Emperor Francis Joseph, his mother the Archduchess Sophie and other members of the Habsburg dynasty. Life at Ischl was very gay with numerous social activities. It was almost a mini-season, and Princess Mary was allowed to attend the *conversazione*, suppers, and balls. One of the highlights for her was to have been asked to dance by the handsome and elegant Austrian Emperor. Moreover for all of her family the Emperor had a special place in their affections and regard. He somehow symbolized the best of the royal traditions and historically he and his dynasty were seen as the protectors of the smaller German states against the obvious ambitions of Prussia. Ischl was also the place for 'the cure' and all generations drank the waters and bathed under the eye of professional medical people. Indeed, 'taking the waters' and homeopathic medicine were very fashionable in royal circles.

The season at Ischl came to an end in early September

when the Emperor Francis Joseph returned to Vienna and the other visitors went home. The Duchess of Cambridge and her daughter followed the imperial family to enjoy the delights of the Austrian capital. They visited galleries and museums which were everywhere, they attended concerts and the theatre as well as having an active social life. Vienna provided as Princess Mary noted 'an endless source of interest and amusement to the visitors'. The Duchess and her party were to be guests of the King of Saxony and en route to Dresden they stopped in Prague for a day where they visited the ex-Emperor Ferdinand and his court but everything was rather dilapidated and the Bohemian capital bore 'the stamp of fallen grandeur'. Arriving in Saxony, Princess Mary and her mother found a number of relations but they did not tarry as it was their intention to get to Strelitz before the winter weather set in. For the Duchess and her daughter and entourage had been travelling for three months and all were desirous of enjoying a more settled existence. Life at Strelitz was relatively unchanged from the days when the Cambridges had visited the town prior to the Duke's death. The Grand-ducal family celebrated Princess Mary's birthday – she was now eighteen – with enthusiasm; this was followed by the Christmas festivities and then a series of balls until early in the new year. There were other entertainments, amateur theatricals, musicals – in one of the latter the princess played in a four-piano arrangement of themes from the opera – as well as those more simple games such as 'Post', 'Hunt the Slipper' and 'Forfeits'. While enjoying her stay in Strelitz the Princess looked forward to her return home; 'dear old England' and Kew were ever in her mind. By the spring of 1852 the family were once again in residence at St James's Palace and Cambridge Cottage.

Although Princess Mary had attended the opening of the Crystal Palace and had made a number of private visits she was not officially 'out'. Her formal presentation to the Queen in late March was to be a sign of her new situation. As a Drawing Room was a very grand affair, Princess Mary's outfit was in keeping. Her dress had 'a train of white moire

Princess Mary Adelaide aged about eighteen years in a portrait by Winterhalter. The latter was a great favourite of Queen Victoria and most of her royal contemporaries. Winterhalter's pictures are generally very flattering to the subject.
(From an engraving in Kinloch Cooke — courtesy John Murray)

H.I.M. Francis Joseph, Emperor of Austria. He and his wife the Empress Elizabeth had acted as Patrons of The Duke of Teck in his youth. The Emperor was always regarded with great respect and affection by the whole of the Teck family.
(From a private collection)

61

antique, trimmed with bugles, and down each side in front, with branches of white roses; the petticoat, white tulle with roses'. On her head were 'two feathers and lappets fastened by turquoise brooches' and she had a 'corsage to match'. The Drawing Room presentation was always an ordeal for any débutante and Princess Mary was aware that after the Queen on this occasion she would be the cynosure of all eyes. When she made her curtsey she did so most gracefully and the Queen gave her a kiss; Princess Mary was as she put it 'into the deep wide world'.

For the next couple of months she enjoyed 'the season, there was a two-day visit to Windsor, several concerts, a dinner for 54 at Angela Burdett-Coutts, a dance at the Duchess of Gloucester's a little hop (my first in London)', two visits to the opera and theatres – her Aunt Kent as chaperone – a dinner and evening party at the Derby's, as well as one at the Jersey's, a court ball – a first also, and a Drawing Room on the Queen's birthday. In addition the Duke of Wellington gave a special ball in her honour which quite delighted her. Indeed she noted that she went to fourteen balls and particularly enjoyed the waltzes. She recorded her partners were all civil and some agreeable. By now she was quite a size and manoeuvring her across the ballroom was quite a feat! The social round ended with the Cup Day at Ascot; for her appearance at the race-course her brother George gave her a 'new gown and bonnet for that occasion!' The gown was 'a lilac *chine*, the bonnet was of *green* crêpe trimmed with bonde and pink roses'. In addition to these rather grand affairs there had been a number of luncheon parties at St James's Palace supervised by her mother. The first season had been a good one but exhausting and she was quite glad to escape to Kew for a rest. After a month in the country the Princess and her mother betook themselves to the Isle of Wight staying for six weeks at Ryde. The summer of 1852 was a particularly dry one and nothing marred the holiday. Princess Mary was as effusive about the Isle of Wight as was Queen Victoria: 'too lovely' and very 'picturesque scenery... so much for admiration'. Indeed she almost wondered why people went abroad when England was so charming.

While they were absent Cambridge Cottage had been undergoing much alteration, the new wing consisting of the public rooms had been found to be in a state of near collapse – evidently they had been very badly constructed in 1840 when the house was enlarged – and consequently required completely rebuilding. The family crammed themselves into the original part of the house but it was very inconvenient and uncomfortable. It was not a very agreeable homecoming and the prospect of living on a builder's site for several months was far from pleasant.

On 14th September the Duke of Wellington died at Walmer Castle. Despite his great age his death was a great shock to everyone. Queen Victoria noted in her journal, 'The death of the Duke of Wellington has deprived the Country of her greatest man, the Crown of its most valuable servant and adviser, the Army of its main strength and support.' These sentiments were shared by her cousin who wrote to her friend Ellinor Napier, 'England has sustained an irreparable loss... this seems universally felt. We, of course, are in mourning.' The demise of the Duke meant that a number of posts suddenly became vacant. The Prime Minister initially thought the Duke of Cambridge might well become the next Commander-in-chief but his military rank was only that of Major-General and he was very young. The Queen sensibly recognized the difficulty and, while she would have liked a member of the royal family to have taken the position, she wrote in her journal, 'He [George] would have carried no weight with the public, and we must not conceal from ourselves that many attacks on the Army which have been sleeping on account of the Duke will now be forthcoming.' The Duke of Cambridge was not forgotten for he was made Ranger of the parks in London and Colonel of the Fusilier Guards. The latter appointment delighted his sister but she was less than enthusiastic about the government's choice of Lord Hardinge as Commander-in-chief. If it could not be her beloved brother

H.R.H. Prince George, Duke of Cambridge in late middle age. Unlike his German relations he generally wore civilian clothes except when acting officially as Commander-in-Chief of the British Army.
(Photograph by Sheppard — Courtesy Longman Group)

she had another candidate: 'I think Lord Hardinge's appointment does not give universal satisfaction, as many wished that
Lord Fitzroy Somerset should get the post, the business of
which he has in point of fact carried on for many years.'
Obviously, of course, her first preference was dear George!

The Victorian revelled in funerals and the Duke's death
provided the perfect occasion for all the display contingent
upon such an event. There were dozens of lengthy notices in
all of the papers and journals, minor poets set the national
grief to verse and there were lengthy eulogies in parliament.
Disraeli rather marred the event by cribbing a speech delivered earlier on a French field marshal and when chided about
it supposedly observed 'one soldier is like another'. However,
all of this was but a prologue to the funeral itself. First came
the lying in state at Chelsea. Princess Mary's own words will
give the proper Victorian tone.

> The sombre appearance of the dimly lighted Hall,
> lined with Grenadiers, their arms reversed, contrasted
> with the illumination of the furthest end where the bier
> stood, behind which rose a laurel wreath encircling *his*
> immortal name, and a curtain of what seemed cloth of
> gold, which *reflected* the light, had a magnificent
> effect; indeed I do not think I ever saw anything better
> done with a view both to appearance and feeling.

For the Princess it was a most affecting scene. Some critics
thought apparently it was 'like a *Chapelle ardente*' but the
Princess with a true protestant view noted, '*I* did not see any
sign of *papacy* anywhere.'

The actual funeral occurred on 18th November. Princess
Mary watched the procession from Gloucester House: 'all
looked so magnificent' and brother 'George commanding
them, so well!' After the procession had passed and the great
lumbering funeral car with the Duke's coffin was on its way to
St Paul's, Princess Mary, her mother and aunt drove to the
church where they were given places of prominence. There

were apparently 16,000 persons present. Officers came from all the regiments of the British army as well as those from the continent, except for the Austrians, who were still irritated by the treatment of General Haynau by a collection of brewers' draymen who had beaten him up because of his bad reputation in Italy. Princess Mary was vastly overwhelmed by everything, 'more impressive than I ever saw before'. She was very upset when the coffin was lowered into its vault and much moved when the whole congregation said the Lord's Prayer. It was obviously '*the nation's heartfelt tribute* of respect to the memory of her *greatest Hero*'.

Following such melancholy reflections and such an emotional outpouring ordinary life might almost be considered mundane but people soon resume their normal patterns of existence and Princess Mary was no exception. For her there were the usual visits to Gloucester House, dinners with the Duke of Cambridge, expeditions to various country houses and the *petits soupers* given by her mother. However, with her birthday – she was now nineteen – the princess began to feel that she was 'terribly old' and that her age was 'quite a serious consideration'.

Despite her lack of money – she had only £3,000 a year voted to her by parliament, Princess Mary was a very eligible young woman for she was a cousin of the Queen of England. Earlier, Prince Henry of the Netherlands had come to England but he made no formal offer. It must be recognised that while her lack of money was a handicap this was not an insurmountable objection for many princesses were equally impoverished and they all found husbands. Princess Mary's difficulty was her size; she was 'a mountain', called by one acquaintance 'a stout party' which was putting it mildly and behind her back Lord Clarendon called her 'our domestic *embonpoint*'. She weighed at least fifteen stone. She was not unattractive, indeed quite the contrary, with good features, lovely hair and dark blue eyes with nice hands and feet. Like many fat people she was graceful in her movements and a good dancer although if one had the misfortune to collide with her and her partner one was likely to be knocked to the floor in a trice. She was intelligent, a lively conversationalist and was quite musical; indeed in Victorian terms she was 'accomplished'. Moreover, she knew how to make the best of her assets and was much interested in clothes and dress. By her easy manner and general affability she was already popular with the general population and she had numerous friends among the aristocracy. However, her immediate marital prospects were not promising and certainly no eligible suitor was readily visible. It was said that no prince was brave enough for such a vast undertaking.

In the late spring of 1853 Emperor Napoleon suddenly had the idea that his cousin Prince Napoleon Jerome, or Plon-Plon as he was nicknamed, might offer his hand to Princess Mary. Earlier the Emperor himself had dallied with the idea of an alliance with Queen Victoria's niece Princess Feodora Hohenlohe but this had come to nothing for the queen was unsympathetic as were the girl's parents and he had married the beautiful Eugenie de Montijo. As yet the imperial couple had no children and Plon-Plon was the heir presumptive. What greater triumph for the House of Bonaparte could be conceived than an alliance with an English princess. The Emperor enquired of his friend Lord Holland how such a proposal might be received. The latter was far from enthusiastic but he took refuge in saying the decision would really rest with Queen Victoria but that it was not likely she would view the matter very positively. However, Holland added when pressed further that the route might well lead through Brussels since it was here that King Leopold lived and he might well be able to exert a positive influence if he could be won over.

When he learned of the idea King Leopold's reponse was distinctly favourable and he agreed to use his good offices. Before he would take any action he thought it would be wise to ascertain Princess Mary's opinions and that of her family. The Emperor and Plon-Plon then requested Lord Henry Lennox, a friend of the Cambridges, to scout out the land. After he visited London he reported, 'The Young lady feebly

The Empress Eugénie, wife of the Emperor Napoleon III, was a great friend of Princess Mary and her family. The picture on the right, circa 1869, is of the Empress when she was living in Paris as a reigning monarch. The picture on the left, circa 1880, is of the Empress as a widow in exile residing in England.
(Picture on left London Stereospic Co.)
(Picture on right by W. D. Downey — private collection)

averse, not personally hostile, but believes the Queen and her mother would never consent'. It is evident that Lord Henry never had any discussion with the Duchess or the matter would have been terminated immediately.

The informal *pourparlers* having been made, Count Walewski consulted his friend Lord Palmerston, the Home Secretary. The latter immediately brought the matter to the attention of Prince Albert. The Home Secretary was enthusiastic basing his arguments on political grounds and, also, as Lord Aberdeen was to note, 'an instance of the infatuation of Lord Palmerston for the cause of Louis Napoleon'. In his letter to Prince Albert, Palmerston stated, 'The young man is said to be good looking, pleasant and intelligent and would be likely to make a better husband than some petty member of a petty German House.' These last comments about minor German royals did nothing to enhance his cause, and created great personal indignation on the part of the Queen. As for Prince Albert, in a memorandum written on 5th November 1853, he was sharply critical of the prospective groom: 'Prince Jerome is the greatest scamp in all France, conspired with the socialists, is not trusted by his cousin, lives a life of profligacy, which has even *disgusted* the French.' Even if Queen Victoria had some reservations about the Cambridges, thinking them frivolous, irresponsible and lacking serious purpose, she was generally fond of 'poor cousin Mary' and was disinclined to sacrifice her happiness for any of Palmerston's pro-French schemes. Moreover she rejected the idea that a refusal might well mean that the Prince would marry a Russian princess and thereby be instrumental in establishing a Russo-French alliance that would endanger the balance of power.

King Leopold of Belgium who had played only a minor role to this point now indicated to his niece that the idea had some merit as it would tie the Emperor to England and in addition ensure Belgian security from any expansionist policies on the part of the French. For once Uncle Leopold was formally put in his place by Windsor and told the whole idea was impossible.

Prince Albert and Queen Victoria suggested to Lord Aberdeen, the Prime Minister, that the Emperor should be informed the marriage could not be considered since the French Prince was a Roman Catholic and Princess Mary was a devout Anglican and a firm Protestant. Aberdeen was enchanted by this approach to the problem and said this was 'by far the best and most effectual mode of putting an end to the subject'.

The French were not to be put off by such a line of argument. Walewski, the ambassador, proceeded to take Lord Clarendon the Foreign Secretary into his confidence, officially informed him of the proposal and added, 'Eh bien, il serait très natural qu'une jeune personne de son age veuille se marier, et le Prince est beau garçon, a une très belle position, qui peut devenir assez brillante un jour. Il y a là assez pour plaire a une jeune dame...' In other words he was trying to bribe the English royal family with the prince's future prospects as an inducement to consent. When Aberdeen was told by his Foreign Secretary of the conversation, he reiterated the sovereign's response and again based a rejection on the question of religion.

At this juncture Prince Albert finally saw fit to tell the Duchess of Cambridge of everything that had occurred since he was convinced she knew nothing of it nor of the very real possibility that Lord Henry Lennox had taken advantage of visiting her house and discussing the matter with Princess Mary without her mother's knowledge. Prince Albert, who always put everything down in writing, recorded, 'She [the Duchess of Cambridge] nearly fainted away at the news and could [hardly] bring herself to realize the possibility of such a project having been seriously entertained; she felt *quite certain* that her daughter could not have been spoken to, or got at by anybody who could have been in on the intrigue and was very much offended that it should have been thought that she or her daughter could have stooped so low, as to be capable of entering upon such a proposal. She knows the young Jerome by *reputation* from his former stays in London and had,

H.I.M. Emperor Napoleon III proposed that his cousin Prince Napoleon marry Princess Mary. The suggestion was rejected by the Cambridge family. Earlier Emperor Napoleon himself had proposed marriage to a cousin of Princess Mary, a Princess von Hohenlohe.
(From a private collection)

during the wars, been robbed and persecuted by the father together with her whole family, when they had to fly from Kassel and the whole of Hesse was ransacked and plundered by him.' Whatever Lord Henry Lennox may have said to Princess Mary, he really cannot have been reporting the truth when he reported her as only being 'feebly averse' because she was devoted to her mother and would have never given any reply without her consent. Indeed, the Duchess did not inform her daughter of Prince Albert's communication and it seems that Princess Mary only discovered the whole business when she read in the *Morning Herald* a despatch purporting to come from Genoa. She was quite angry and, as Clarendon said to Walewski, 'She had deeply resented, first, the idea that any marriage could be made for her without her knowledge, next, that the marriage should be with a Roman Catholic, and lastly, that the suitor could be a man of character so notoriously bad that she herself was aware of it'.

Despite the failure of Walewski and his friend Lord Palmerston, the Emperor refused to be daunted. He brought up the matter anew to Lord Cowley, the British ambassador, in late November. He trotted out the Palmerston argument that the marriage would give the lie to the idea that the Anglo-French entente was really insubstantial. Cowley was amazed and more so when the Emperor suggested that Plon-Plon should actually visit England and meet Princess Mary. The ambassador who hitherto had no knowledge of the whole affair took a determined stand saying that the religious question was such that it could not be overcome: no English princess had ever married a Roman Catholic. Then he added, taking advantage of his friendship with the Emperor, that Prince Napoleon 'did not bear the best of reputations'.

All the while King Leopold of Belgium continued to press the Bonaparte case calling Princess Mary 'our fat Iphégénie' and likened the idea of the marriage to the sacrifice of the latter to Artemis. Queen Victoria was much irritated with her uncle; he was obviously being obtuse and a catspaw for French ambitions, and she was sharply critical when she wrote,

> I must say dearest Uncle, that I *cannot* for the moment *comprehend* how you can wish for *such* a disgrace... I share George's [the Duke of Cambridge's] feelings that it is a *great* insult to his sister as a lady and princess of England.... Poor Mary herself has been perfectly furious at the mention of it in the papers. It is, however, *enterre*, and I pray we may never hear of it again.

King Leopold was tempoarily silenced by his niece's rebuke but did not let the matter entirely die and tried on at least two subsequent occasions. Queen Victoria's responses to both allusions were equally tart and she expressed herself surprised and annoyed that he should have revived the matter. On these occasions 'dearest Uncle' was decidedly out of his niece's favour. Despite all efforts to keep the matter from the world, 'the royal mob' were *au courant* of the project. Queen Sophie of the Netherlands wrote to her friend, Lady Malet, 'I had a letter from the Duchess of Cambridge. On purpose to tell me, I am not to believe a word of a marriage between her daughter and my cousin, Napoleon – but this fat girl is twenty-one and no husband.' Evidently, the Cambridges were still very concerned that their relations might actually believe the impossible was possible.

The matter was formally ended with the British royal family's total rejection of the proposal. The Emperor had to accept the fact that there could be no marriage alliance between his family and that of Queen Victoria. England and France may have been allies for good sound political reasons but such friendship did not mean that Queen Victoria wanted a Bonaparte and certainly not one like Plon–Plon as a cousin.

The sentiments of Prince Napoleon are not known but certainly he was no broken-hearted swain. For the next half dozen years he continued his raffish existence. In 1859 he married Princess Clothilde, the daughter of King Victor Emmanuel of Piedmont. This was strictly the result of a political decision and related directly to French policy in Italy. Princess Clothilde was the ideal sort of wife for the prince, pious and unassuming; she accepted her husband for what he was; she was without illusions. But after the fall of the Second Empire she remained loyal to him. From their children were to descend the modern-day claimants to the imperial title.

While all of these complicated negotiations were in process England and France had become allies in the war against Russia. Princess Mary was very much caught up in the anti-Russian sentiment and was extremely jingoistic. She was vastly pleased when she learned that her brother was to command the First Division, although this would mean he would be on active service in the Crimea and far from the family. To celebrate his appointment, his mother and sister gave a dinner in his honour and one of the principal guests was Lord Raglan, who was in charge of the entire British contingent of two divisions and under whom the Duke of Cambridge would serve. Amidst floods of tears and lamentations by his mother and younger sister, the Duke made his adieux on 10th April 1854. 'We all broke down at the last' and for the next twelve months the family wrote to him constantly and anxiously awaited his replies. Princess Mary, normally an indifferent and never an enthusiastic correspondent – she was often in disgrace with the Queen because of her failure to answer letters – took it upon herself to give her absent brother all the news. A stream of letters went to the front recounting court life, country house visits, theatrical performances and family gossip.

Owing to the war there were no expeditions to Rumpenheim and Strelitz. At the close of the season, Princess Mary and her mother retired to Kew for the summer. The Princess's journal is filled with news of the war and of announcements of casualties especially of family friends. With each victory the Princess would report, 'Well may we feel proud of our noble countrymen' and the most noble was, of course, her brother.

The Duke was present at the Battle of Inkerman and while

H.R.H. Princess Clotilde of Savoy, the daughter of King Victor Emmanuel II. She married Prince Napoleon who at one time was a suitor of Princess Mary. The latter's hand was sought by her father, so the English princess would have been the mother-in-law of a man who wished to marry her himself.
(Photograph by M. Rosati — courtesy Madame Grillo Pasquarelli)

a ball grazed his arm, he was not wounded largely because the ball was deflected by two buttons ornamented with the hair of his mother and sister. The latter observed on learning of the event, 'Is it not *that* touching?' However his exertions and a fever caused him to be sent to recuperate on the *Retribution*. This enforced rest almost resulted in his being drowned as a dreadful storm came up and drove a number of vessels on to the rocky shore with a loss of all aboard. The *Retribution* successfully manged to escape destruction and the Duke survived. His general state did not improve, and he was ordered back to Constantinople where he resided at the British Embassy. His fever did not abate even in these more comfortable surroundings and the Duke applied for leave to return home on the grounds of continued ill health. His request was granted but the decision was not greeted in all quarters with much enthusiasm. It was thought that he ought to have remained since he was not desperately ill and many others were in a far worse situation. Indeed, some critics even implied that the Duke's action was almost a form of desertion. Of course, his sister did not share such opinion; to her he was a hero. On 30th January he was in London: 'At a quarter to seven [in the evening],' Princess Mary wrote, 'the dear brave fellow (*our hero*) made his appearance. It was a *happy* moment.'

A few days later she wrote again, 'George is daily regaining strength thanks to "dear old England"... but he certainly looks pulled down.... He has grown much thinner, and *we* think much handsomer as his features are quite pointed, and moreover, set off to great advantage by a splendid beard, to which I have quite lost my heart.' The Duke was soon quite recovered, resumed his military duties in London, and his domestic life with Louisa. It was almost as if he had never been away, but he had seen action and to the female members of the family he was 'quite the hero'.

The event of the spring of 1855 was not the demise of the Tsar, though his death certainly hastened the end of the war, but the visit of Napoleon and his wife to Windsor. This state visit was the public acknowledgement by the British of their acceptance of the empire and of the alliance. Of course, the Emperor had been in London before. He had lived in the city while in exile and just prior to his return to France in 1848 he had been a special constable during the Chartist demonstrations. He had many friends in England, though some to be sure were unlikely to win the approbation of the Queen and Prince Albert and were not included in any part of the official programme. For Eugénie this was her first foreign appearance as Empress of France and everyone was curious to see the beautiful Spaniard for whom Napoleon had eschewed an alliance with a royal family. Everyone knew of her great beauty and she did not disappoint. The Emperor on the other hand was less impressive, short in stature, heavy in build, and decidedly unhandsome with his waxed mustachios and his languid eyes. What he lacked in looks he made up in an ability to charm. On his meeting with Queen Victoria he flirted with her outrageously but so subtly she was enchanted. Indeed, the imperial couple made an excellent impression on their host and hostess, and they all became firm friends.

During the imperial couple's sojourn at Windsor, Princess Mary was invited to meet them and attended 'the grand banquet in their honour... given in St George's Hall'. It was a very splendid occasion with seventy-six guests sitting down to dinner and all *en grand tenue*, as one guest reported. After the banquet was over, there was a ball in the Waterloo Gallery. Princess Mary liked dancing but with her there was always an element of danger. This time, however, there were no misadventures. On another occasion at Twickenham, when taking part in the Lancers, she collided with another girl and knocked her flat on the floor.

The next day she breakfasted with the Emperor, made a morning call on the Empress and then lunched with the Queen and her guests. In the afternoon Princess Mary was one of the privileged spectators in the throne room when Napoleon was given the Garter. The day concluded with another large banquet. Princess Mary left Windsor the next morning as did the imperial party accompanied by the Queen and Prince Albert. For the next two days Napoleon and Eugénie and their host and hostess were at Buckingham Palace. Princess Mary was again in attendance, this time at the Grand Concert. When the musical entertainment was over, Princess Mary bade the Emperor and Empress adieu and drove back to Kew where she did not arrive until 2 a.m. She summarized the visit most aptly: 'The visit of the Emperor and Empress has gone off very well indeed, thanks to his tact and agreeable cleverness, and her pleasing and unassuming manners.' Evidently Napoleon exerted himself to be charming to the Queen's stout cousin despite her refusal to marry a Bonaparte. Her remarks about Eugénie are slightly droll: evidently she seems to have expected somebody who was not of royal birth to find it difficult to cope with such a situation and almost surprised that the Empress managed so well.

One result of this meeting was a proposal made the following year by Eugénie concerning Princess Mary. The Empress suggested that as the Princess was now twenty-two, a marriage might be arranged between her and Prince Oscar of Sweden. He was a few years her senior, the second son of the king, and as he had an elder brother it was unlikely that he would succeed to the throne. It seemed from the viewpoint of Paris that this marriage would be a practical one from all aspects. The Houses of Bernadette and Bonaparte were related and this marriage if it took place would give the latter a connection, albeit a distant one, with the British royal family. If Napoleon III could not succeed in getting Princess Mary for Plon-Plon he might at least have her marry another of his cousins. Queen Victoria, who was informed of the idea in a letter from Eugénie, sensibly suggested the two young people meet. The Prince came to England in the summer of 1856. He met Princess Mary on several occasions but did not propose. He went on to Paris where apparently he informed Eugénie that he was disinclined to marry Princess Mary. No reason for his refusal was ever given but he was possibly put off by her rather casual manner – the German royals found this very irksome – and also her vast size. If he were concerned to have a family this could have been a very real consideration for it was then believed that fat women had difficulties in childbirth. There the matter ended. The next year he married Princess Sophie of Nassau. In 1872 he became King of Sweden. Thus, Princess Mary lost the chance of being a consort to a reigning monarch. She would have done well in the role and probably would have been a popular queen.

In the late winter of 1855 another royal visitor and ally in the war with Russia arrived. This new guest was Victor Emmanuel of Savoy – a short, swarthy-looking man with great mustachios and a reputation that was earthy. Ballerinas were his specialty and whenever he attended a performance of the ballet, equerries were kept as busy as the postman delivering notes to preferred young damsels propositioning them in a very flagrant fashion. The king's peccadillos were well known, at least to the male sex, and were generally tolerated. At a young age he had married one of those innumerable Habsburg archduchesses, in this case Marie Adelaide the daughter of Archduke Rainier, but his wife's Austrian connections did not prevent him from promoting a policy directed toward that country's withdrawal from its Italian possessions. Once again, Princess Mary was invited to be a member of the party to welcome a royal guest. There was another enormous gala dinner for ninety persons in St George's Hall with Princess Mary seated next to Count Cavour, the Sardinian prime minister. The next day she attended a breakfast with the Sardinian monarch. – all very informal and *en famille* – and was present in the evening at a second banquet. On this latter occasion Princess Mary had a place of honour sitting next to the King himself. King Victor Emmanuel, like the Emperor Napoleon, was given the Garter and the Cambridges were all interested spectators. Princess Mary's comments on the Sardinian visit are interesting: 'His visit has been quite an affair of state and grandeur. In this pageantry His Majesty must have found himself rather out of place, as he is naturally very shy, which he conceals under a brusque manner. He is also far from prepossessing in appearance.' She did add, however, that he was 'remarkably soldier-like, frank, and I believe, clever'.

By now King Victor Emmanuel was a widower, his wife having died the previous January, and apparently after meeting Princess Mary he was rather impressed by her. At the same time he very obviously thought an alliance with the British Crown might be politically advantageous. Earlier, prior to the state visit, Baron Marochetti, the well-known and fashionable sculptor who spent much time in England, had considered Princess Mary as a possible consort for his sovereign. Nine months after the king's visit, Cavour asked Marochetti to act as his agent in putting forward a formal offer of marriage. Princess Mary and her mother were on the continent when the offer arrived; it was sent at once to the Duchess of Cambridge and her daughter who were at Baden. The Duchess was opposed to the idea totally, being convinced that her daughter would be poisoned by the Jesuits and regarded 'as a sort of Anne Boleyne'. Princess Mary's rejection was immediate. She was a devout and sincere Anglican. She had been very distressed when her friend Eleanor Draper Berry had become a Roman Catholic, observing, 'My heart is truly Protestant' and

Pray admire my John Bull feelings.... I shall never become a disciple of yours. I leave you to the *Italian* school; whilst I retain my own dear country *and her church*, to which I pray God I may ever cling with a *true Protestant heart.*

She simply could not conceive of such an alliance, asking her brother, 'How would the announcement of the marriage of an English princess (a Guelph) with a papist Sovereign be taken by John Bull?' The British public had only a few years earlier expressed its anti-catholicism in its reaction to what was called 'papal aggression' when Pope Pius IX had restored the Roman Catholic hierarchy. The Lord Chancellor on that occasion had

H.R.H. The Princess Mary of Cambridge.

After a drawing by Lombardi of Princess Mary in her early twenties, this portrait is more life-like than the romanticized one painted by his contemporary Winterhalter a few years previously. Carte de visite.
(From Kinloch Cooke — courtesy John Murray)

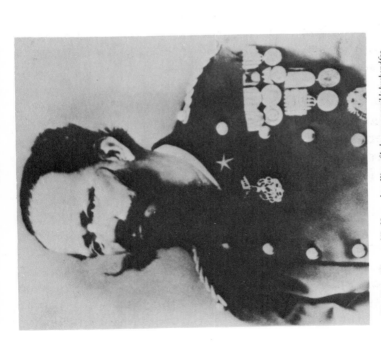

King Victor Emmanuel II of Savoy, later King of Italy, was a possible husband for Princess Mary. The latter declined to marry the Italian monarch and her mother observed that as a protestant the Princess would have been regarded as 'a sort of Anne Boleyn' in Turin.
(From a private collection)

observed, 'Under our feet we'll stamp the Cardinal's hat, in spite of Pope or dignitaries in Church'. There were critical articles in *The Times* and Cardinal Wiseman and the Bishop of Rome were burned in effigy. John Bull's feelings were all too well known. Nobody was much surprised by the reaction of the princess.

However the proprieties had to be observed. The Duke of Cambridge forwarded his sister's letter to the Queen; another in a similar vein was sent to Windsor by Lord Clarendon, who had also received a communication from Baden. The Duke of Cambridge heartily concurred in the correctness of his sister's response as did Queen Victoria. She wrote to the duke saying the letter was 'admirably written' and did 'dear Mary the greatest credit'. It put the matter 'on the right ground, viz. that of the *Protestant* feeling which should always actuate our family', adding, 'I am very glad that the decision has been so entirely dear Mary's own and that she is convinced of my anxious work for her happiness and welfare.'

Lord Clarendon, who had not expected a contrary view – indeed, he had so indicated his feelings to Marochetti – put the matter very tactfully to the Sardinian emissary. After extolling King Victor Emmanuel and his character he went on to say, 'Her Royal Highness feels that as the Protestant Queen of Sardinia she must be in a false position, and that a wife can never find herself thus placed without injury to her husband... she feels that she would be the object of constant suspicion, that her motives would be liable to misconstruction and that the King would be exposed to grave embarrassments, which time would only serve to increase.' Clarendon also included all of those necessary phrases such as 'many excellent and noble qualities' of Victor Emmanuel to make the rejection easier to accept. The consequence of this refusal of the offer of marriage was aptly summarized by Queen Victoria: 'It effectively closes... the door to *all Catholic* proposals – whether from Kings or Princes', thereby limiting the circle of prospective spouses for Princess Mary, and making things less political in the future.

A month later Princess Mary had yet another proposal. This occurred at Rumpenheim, where a minor German princeling enquired from her uncle the Landgraf of Hesse if he might offer his hand in marriage. The Landgraf received the proposition politely, made the suitable diplomatic reply on behalf of his niece but said, quite firmly, 'No'. Thus terminated all immediate possibilities of a marriage for Princess Mary. Indeed, over the next few years she joked about being 'a jolly old maid' but she cannot have contemplated the future with great equanimity having observed the rather dull and dreary lives of her elderly aunts the daughters of George III. Her relations never despaired of finding her a husband and one of the perennial topics appearing in the correspondence of her royal connections is 'what to do about poor Mary'.

The root of the problem was that Princess Mary was in an intolerable position. First, she was not rich with only a modest income from parliament for her life. Queen Victoria observed of another poor princess, Princess Adelaide of Saxe-Meiningen, a

> poor girl has not much free choice, a good party presents itself; if she does not dislike the man and if her parents like it, why if she refuses him she runs the risk of getting no husband at all, and we see by poor cousin Mary, what the consequences of that is. For a princess – a very sad, bad lookout!

Secondly, she was not what was thought to be attractive – good looking, yes – but as King Leopold observed 'grown out of compass'. Her size and also her informality were rather offputting. Queen Victoria, who was very small in stature, needed all of her regal presence to cope with her stout cousin who had the facility of rather overwhelming people. In an age which demanded that women be rather self-effacing and delicate, Princess Mary simply did not fit the mould. Queen Sophie summed up the case: 'Princess Mary is a spoiled child, spoiled by popularity I never understood, except she is popu-

lar because she is fat and looks so good-humoured but is not.
The mob likes fat people, thinks them good natured which is
quite wrong.... Princess Mary is very impertinent.' The Germans in particular found it dismaying. 'She laughed and
talked a deal', as her young cousin Victoria of Prussia noted,
or as the Queen put it more explicitly her 'manners... and
conversation... are not refined'.

Indeed, she was more at ease with the aristocracy and it
was believed that she was very fond of several young peers.
Among those whose names were passed about in society were
the Dukes of Rutland and Newcastle, and Lords Canterbury
and Hood, but the prospect of marriage with any of these was
firmly rejected by Queen Victoria, who believed it would
have been impossible for her to maintain her royal position.
Ironically, this difficulty was not recognized when Princess
Louise chose to marry Lord Lorne some years later. Yet
Queen Victoria could say on one occasion, 'I always think she
will marry some German *Kammerherr* or Young Officer. It
would really be the best thing.' Obviously the problem of
rank was not to the Queen a major drawback if her stout
cousin were in Germany. Indeed several princesses did marry
outside their circle in Germany. For example, a Württemberg
princess was the wife of Count Niepperg while a princess of
Schleswig-Holstein married a professor from Hamburg.
Finally part of the problem was Princess Mary's mother, the
Duchess of Cambridge, who while saying she wanted her
daughter to marry was at the same time quite content to have
her for a companion. In many households one daughter devoted her life to her parents and was warmly applauded by
society for doing so. Evidently prospective suitors were re-
buffed by the Duchess of Cambridge herself – not, of course,
officially for the reason that she wished to retain her daughter
as a companion. Queen Victoria was to take a similar stance
with respect to Princess Beatrice and when the latter did
finally marry Prince Henry of Battenberg it was only
approved after the young couple agreed to reside permanently
with the bride's mother. Rather, the Duchess justified her

H.M. Queen Sophie of the Netherlands was a friend of the Cambridge family. She was delighted when Prince Francis married Princess Mary. She was not prey to the concern about differences of rank that troubled so many of her royal relations.
(From a painting by Winterhalter in the collection of H.M. Queen Beatrix of the Netherlands)

opposition on the grounds that she simply found nothing to persuade her this or that young prince would be suitable. It seemed as if 'poor Mary' was doomed to be an old maid unless some younger son with limited prospects in his own country came forward and agreed to live at least partly in England.

With the question of a husband for Princess Mary unresolved, life in St James's Palace and at Kew continued in its accustomed pattern. There were the small dinners at Cambridge Cottage, the receptions at Gloucester House given by the Duchess of Gloucester, the visits to Windsor and the sojourns in various country houses with the nobility.

In the spring of 1856 the Duchess of Cambridge appointed a new lady-in-waiting who was to be her companion for three decades. This addition to the Cambridge ménage was Lady Geraldine Somerset, a year older than Princess Mary and the daughter of the Duke of Beaufort. Lady Geraldine was to be a sort of malevolent Greek chorus in the later life of Princess Mary, whom she grew to dislike intensely and to regard as a monster of selfishness and self-indulgence. Comments such as 'beslobbering and beslavering the vile *Diablesse*' and others more malicious appear in her diary. Lady Geraldine's affections were centred on the Duke of Cambridge – it was a case of unrequited love – and for him nothing was too good, no praise sufficient. The consequence was that she was totally uncharitable to most other people: to the widowed Duchess she was loyal and dutiful but not loving; and Princess Mary and later her daughter, Princess May, were viewed always critically and when weighed in the balance were always found wanting. Princess Mary was quite oblivious to her mother's lady-in-waiting's rather spiteful outlook on life and 'Geraldo' as she called her is always referred to with affection. Lady Geraldine's ill temper and disagreeable outlook were to cause Princess Mary a certain amount of trouble over the years but the latter seems to have been oblivious of the source of her difficulties. Even the Duke of Teck was aware of the ill nature of Lady Geraldine and commented, 'Poor Geraldine, she really looked after the boys and me, but May was a thorn in her eye and she had a diabolical hate against Mary'. But this was all in the future. Indeed, Lady Geraldine's appointment was greeted with enthusiasm by Princess Mary, who conducted her to Buckingham Palace for inspection by Queen Victoria and who evidently found her very good company. Lady Geraldine was to be of the party when the annual summer expedition to Rumpenheim was arranged; not for her was to be a role of 'not really being in the way' and 'not being seen much', which was the ideal of royal personages of their attendants. Lady Geraldine was a very visible individual.

The summer expedition to the continent began in mid-August; after a stormy crossing they reached Calais where they passed the night. Early in the morning they took the train to Cologne and transferred to a boat for the journey up the Rhine. The Duchess of Cambridge's carriage was just put aboard the steamer and she sat in it for much of the journey, even taking a sort of picnic luncheon on it as well. Their destination was Mainz and then Baden to be followed by a lengthy sojourn at Rumpenheim. This was to be the first of a number of visits that Lady Geraldine would make to the beloved holiday house. She was to find 'the royal mob' to be infinitely more cosy and casual than had been her experience in England but the informality and lack of concern she found infuriating. Over the years Rumpenheim was to have too many people milling about doing nothing constructive, concerned only for childish games and without any redeeming features. The food was uneatable and the people were boring. Lady Geraldine seems never to have understood or appreciated that 'the royal mob' found Rumpenheim almost perfect because they could be themselves and not as she would always have them, the perfect or potentially perfect social models for their subjects. Strelitz on the other hand was another matter; Lady Geraldine found it more to her taste. The old-fashioned formality of the court and its denizens, all of whom knew their places precisely, were always properly dressed for every occasion and were not inclined to the lapses of propriety that pervaded everyone and everything at Rumpenheim. Moreov-

The Schloss at Neu Strelitz was the home of the sister and brother-in-law of Princess Mary. The latter and her family were frequent visitors. Lady Geraldine Somerset, lady-in-waiting to the Duchess of Cambridge, much preferred Neu Strelitz to Rumpenheim.
(Collection Staatsarchiv Schwerin)

er, life at the court of Mecklenburg-Strelitz was ordered, there was time for every event. The walks were conducted in a dignified manner – no wild running about – the expeditions to neighbouring castles were of suitable duration and never exhausting. In addition, the rulers of Mecklenburg-Strelitz insisted on proper meals, never as at Rumpenheim 'too infamous... *pas mangeable'*. In sum, Neu Strelitz provided the suitable ambience for court life as Lady Geraldine and others of her ilk assumed it ought to be.

To the 'royal mob' Rumpenheim was paradisaical for just the opposite reasons that Strelitz was correct in Lady Geraldine's view. It was totally ideal for a holiday and it was the base for expeditions to see the sights and to pass the time with the extended family circle. Indeed, the sudden meetings with family connections often quite unexpectedly provided one of the pleasures of continental travel. Moreover, even the poorest of princes seemed to have plenty of space to accommodate the visitors and to provide suitable entertainment even if it only consisted of a dinner, gossip and music or round games.

Rumpenheim was essentially a holiday house and by October everyone was ready to return home. For the Cambridges this was London but first there was as always the difficulty of the Channel crossing and the Duchess anticipated a dreadful few hours. However, in this autumn when they reached Calais they were assured that there would be no problems, that it would be 'a lovely passage', and for once it was. It took only an hour-and-a-half and as Princess Mary recorded in her journal, 'It was an excellent passage.... Everybody [read the Duchess of Cambridge] kept well.' While foreign travel was pleasant enough it was vastly agreeable to be home again and Princess Mary, ever a loyal Englishwoman, observed about their first meal at Kew, 'How delicious the English fare seemed to us all, after having lived two months abroad!' These sentiments have been shared by many of her fellow countrymen who have deplored 'foreign messes' – that is, French food and sauces – and regretted the lack of a good cup of tea in foreign parts.

After every holiday the first visit made by the Cambridges was to Gloucester House to see 'dearest Aunt Mary'. When they had departed they were concerned about her general state of health but she appears to have coped well in their absence and even looked 'better and more *rajeunie*... than could have... [been] hoped'. A welcome and happy event indeed. The Duchess and her daughter could now resume their daily lives with a sense of equanimity and 'in the full conviction that however charming and agreeable there's no place like home'.

Despite the impression gained by Princess Mary that her aunt, the Duchess of Gloucester, was in reasonable health it was actually quite the reverse. The old princess was very frail. The jolly gathering of the family and friends at Gloucester House on Christmas night 1856 (and with it the usual festivities and tree) was to be the last of such celebrations.

In the spring the Duchess of Gloucester's health took a turn for the worse. The whole family took turns at her bedside. The invalid's eighty-first birthday was not kept as it would have been in the past as she was too unwell. However, Princess Mary and her brother were allowed to visit the patient's bedroom and give their special greetings. The aged princess was well enough to recognize her visitors and their presence and obvious affection appeared to give her pleasure. For once the Princess Augusta actually arrived before the patient died. She was recognized by the old lady who seemed generally delighted to see her.

The last day in the life of the sole surviving child of George III might serve as a model for all Victorian death bed scenes. On 29th April the Duke of Cambridge sent for his mother and sisters and upon their arrival they found 'her hours were numbered, it was a *sad, sad,* scene. Tears were on every face.... On their raising the much loved patient... she half unclosed her eyes but the *sight* seemed *gone.*' Princess Mary left the room accompanied by the others who listened to a reading by a lady-in-waiting on 'meditations on the approach of death'. The Duchess of Kent was the next to arrive and after seeing the patient 'was much overcome'. Prince Albert and his eldest son made their appearance. The latter went to the bedside and kissed the dying woman's brow, a typical gesture of courtesy and affection and very much in keeping with his personality. The Queen did not come because she was recovering from the birth of Princess Beatrice and it was thought that the whole business would be too fatiguing and possibly dangerous to her health.

The Cambridges and the whole household prepared themselves for the end which was imminent by early evening. They did not leave the house but went and lay on sofas until summoned. Finally they were told to come at once and around the bed were fifteen persons who knelt in tears while prayers were said. The vigil lasted some two hours. Death came at a quarter past five in the morning. At that point a stifled sob broke from all present. An hour later the Cambridge family retired to Kew but after a short sojourn and getting out their mourning clothes were back at noon to view the corpse. To have 'one more look at that dear inanimate face... alas how we missed that sweet smile of welcome she *always* gave us'. After departing from Gloucester House in a closed carriage they went to the palace to see the Queen and her husband, and before leaving London made a call on the Duchess of Kent. As Princess Mary observed of the deceased, 'We young people, that is to say George, Augusta and I loved her as a second mother!'

The Duke of Cambridge was in charge of the funeral which took place at Windsor. To those present it was 'beautifully impressive and not a dry eye was to be found in the Church'. The Duke was her principal legatee, receiving Gloucester House and its contents; here he was to reside until his death in 1904 but he never really made full use of that handsome and elegant residence confining himself to only a few rooms because he had his other and more personal residence with his 'dear Louisa'. Princess Mary inherited a goodly quantity of jewellery and silver; as the Duke commented, 'It is a beautiful will, not anybody forgotten.'

Because of the death of her aunt and the requirements for court mourning, Princess Mary and her mother saw little of society for some months. Indeed, they did not really emerge from their self-imposed seclusion until the autumn. However, in mourning or not, the expedition to Rumpenheim was not to be put off; besides, a sojourn with her own dear Hessian relations would do much to cheer up the spirits of the Duchess and her daughter. So much better did the royal ladies feel after a holiday in Rumpenheim they decided to spend some time in Paris. They saw all the sights like good tourists but since they were still in mourning they did not participate in any official functions and seem to have studiously avoided the imperial court. Despite these limitations Princess Mary thoroughly enjoyed her stay in Paris but she was, as she observed, 'far too John Bullish to think that gay pleasure hunting city at all to be compared with dear grand old London'.

Princess Mary was now twenty-four and no thinner. The American minister thought her 'very fat, very thick set' and weighing two hundred and fifty pounds. Even Queen Victoria could not hide from herself the fact that her cousin was very stout and wrote when a young prince was a potential suitor the Princess Mary was 'plus forte que la plupart des jeunes dames de son age', and with no settled prospects. Hence news of the engagement of her young second cousin the Princess Royal to Prince Frederick of Prussia can only have been received with mixed feelings for the bride to be was only sixteen. Of course Princess Mary wished the young couple much happiness but she cannot have failed to contemplate and compare her own situation with chagrin and gloom.

Princess Victoria was an interesting and lively young woman, highly intelligent and extremely well-educated. She was very much her father's child and definitely his favourite. Undoubtedly, Prince Albert hoped that an alliance between the royal families of England and Prussia would have happy consequences. The Prince was an ardent advocate of German unification and he believed that Prussia was the logical leader but he recognized that the house of Hohenzollern was not

H.R.H. Princess Victoria, Princess Royal and later German Empress, the eldest daughter of Queen Victoria, was much admired by the Tecks for her charm and her intellectual attainments. Happy in her marriage, she was frustrated in her efforts to liberalize German policies.
(From a private collection)

famous for liberal ideas. To be sure King Frederick William IV had been forced to grant a constitution in 1848 but he had done so under duress and the traditions of the country and its rulers were conservative. Prince Albert had great hopes for Prince Frederick William and he thought that with the Princess Victoria as his wife it would strengthen his belief in liberalism and parliamentary government. Having such principles, a united Germany could not fail to be a happy and prosperous country. Regretfully, what Prince Albert anticipated did not ensue; to be sure the prince and princess were ideally happy in their domestic situation but were forced to stand on the sidelines and observe how Prussia and, later, the German Empire failed to become a liberal state.

Princess Victoria was married on 25th January; for a fortnight before there was a gaggle of foreign guests arriving in London. Originally the Prussians had proposed that the marriage take place in Berlin but Queen Victoria had nipped the idea in the bud, observing that 'it was not every day that a Prussian prince married the eldest daughter of the Queen of England'. There were the usual ceremonial calls. One afternoon the Duchess and her daughter received Princes Frederick Charles, Frederick Albert and Adalbert of Prussia as well as the Duke of Saxe-Coburg and Prince Hohenzollern. There were dinners – on 18th January sixty-nine persons sat down for a meal at the palace – and receptions, balls and galas at the opera and the theatre. Princess Mary attended everything and met everybody. The foreign dignitaries were impressed by her affability and her *joie de vivre*, and while they admired her looks they were taken aback by her size. However, in the words of one of the 'royal mob', 'her bright manner and becoming smiles won all hearts.'

Princess Mary was not a member of the bridal party but was in the royal procession. Naturally, the Prince and Princess of Prussia, the parents of the groom, were prominent. So was the Duke of Saxe-Coburg, the bride's uncle. The English royal family followed their many guests. Princess Mary, attended by Arabella West, and the Duchess of Cambridge with Lady Geraldine were very much to the fore as they made their way through the corridors of St James's Palace to the Chapel Royal where the wedding was to take place. Indeed, Princess Mary actually led in the British contingent. Following the ceremony there were the usual signing of the register and a wedding breakfast for the family. With the departure of the young couple to Windsor for their honeymoon the day came to an end but four days later they joined the royal family at the opera and all were received with great enthusiasm. When Prince Frederick and Princess Victoria finally took their leave from the latter's family, it was, as Princess Mary recorded in her journal, '*A very gloomy tearful day! At 11:30 we drove to the Palace to see poor dear Vicky off... and found dear Victoria surrounded by a number of crying relations in the Queen's Closet*'. But such an emotional scene was not untypical and in its way was almost a form of enjoyment.

Nowhere does Princess Mary record feeling envy for her young cousin's bright prospects but at twenty-five she cannot but have paused now and again to contemplate her own position. As she was to confess to her brother, being an old maid was not a happy prospect and she saw for herself the 'gloomy dreams of an old-maidish future, coupled with a homely and dreary position'.

*H.I.H. Crown Prince Rudolph of Austria-Hungary was a friend of The Duke of Teck. The Crown Prince led a wildlife,
neglected his wife and ultimately committed suicide at Mayerling with his mistress The Countess Maria Vatsera. The
scandal shocked 'the royal mob'.*
(From a private collection)

CHAPTER THREE

'Strong, Dark Blood'

With the Princess Royal well and safely settled, Queen Victoria could contemplate anew the problem of 'poor Mary' and almost as soon as her daughter was settled in Berlin she began an active correspondence on the subject. As she said, 'You know how anxious we are... George constantly asking me if there is no one.... Now do see what you and dear Fritz can do.' The matter exercised Princess Mary's German relations as well; to everyone she was a source of embarrassment as well as being a sad case.

Once put to the test the family found a number of potential spouses for the princess. The first candidate put forward was Gustave of Saxe-Weimar, a nephew of Queen Adelaide and brother of the Duke of Cambridge's great friend Prince Edward who lived in England. For some reason unspecified – perhaps it was his age, he was fifty-one – the Duchess of Cambridge rejected him outright. The Duchess seems to have favoured Prince Albert of Prussia, known to the family as Abbat, who was later a candidate advanced by Princess Victoria as a husband for one of her sisters, but for Princess Mary Prince Albert was thought to be too young and of the wrong temperament. From several sources Queen Victoria heard of Augustus of Württemberg as an excellent choice and of a suitable age, namely forty-five, for Princess Mary had said she preferred an older man 'which from her size and her free manner' the Queen believed 'would be much more appropriate than a young man'. Prince Augustus had other merits as well; not only was he virtuous but more importantly from the Cambridge point of view he was ' a very fine-looking man'. This candidate was vetoed by the Crown Princess of Prussia who observed of him that he was 'in no respect to be recommended... in my humble opinion or that of Fritz.' On receiving this negative reaction the Queen now changed her views as well and hastened to defend herself by noting that Prince Hohenzollern had put Prince Augustus forward since there seemed no other viable candidate and he was the last possibility. The Queen had come to the position of thinking any husband would suffice because 'poor Mary' was 'desperate and bitter'. Having failed to find a suitable prospect, 'the royal mob' as well as Queen Victoria shelved the problem for the moment. Periodically discreet enquiries were made on behalf of Roman Catholic princes – evidently there were more of them – and Princess Victoria sounded out her mother on several occasions as to her feelings. Queen Victoria made it clear that a Roman Catholic was out of the question and the more so since Victor Emmanuel had been rejected on those grounds despite his 'toleration in religion and against the Pope'. No Roman Catholic would be considered.

A new candidate emerged in the Duke of Brunswick. He was firmly protestant and closely related to the House of Hanover. Indeed the duchy ultimately descended to the grandson of the last King of Hanover. Theoretically he was most suitable. However, the Duke showed no inclination for the marriage; he was somewhat eccentric in any case and would probably not have been very reliable. 'Poor Mary' remained unwed. 'I fear there is no hope for a husband,' was the Queen's plaintive comment. Nevertheless Queen Victoria did not abandon her quest. Another Prussian, Prince George, came into view briefly as the candidate of the Princess Victoria, his chief disadvantage being his poor health. He quickly removed himself from the stakes by making a morganatic marriage as had another potential Prussian prince somewhat earlier. To the despair of the matchmakers the House of Hohenzollern's princelings apparently chose domestic happiness over royal rank. Queen Sophie of the Netherlands took the gloomiest views of 'poor Mary's' prospects and wrote to her friend Lady Malet, 'Poor Princess Mary. I pity her and no doubt she will end as her aunts did – a child and no husband' an obvious allusion to the gossip about Princesses Sophia and

Amelia, the daughters of George III, who were supposed to have had liaisons with gentlemen of the court since their parents declined to let them marry.

By this time Princess Mary was twenty-eight and her prospects were dim indeed. Maurice of Altenburg, who seemed a very real candidate, had decided to marry a princess of Saxe-Meiningen. This evoked from Queen Victoria, 'Alas poor Mary! I really am in despair about it! It is all her mother's fault for she should have taught her better manners.' This last remark relates to Princess Mary's 'forward manner' and being 'fearfully pleasure-seeking' which put people off. On the other hand, this vivacity was not seen by all as a deterrent; Queen Sophie of the Netherlands felt that Princess Mary could 'put life into anything and anyone if she chooses'. While she recommended a rather dull Prince William of Baden, she recognized it would have been a case of 'fire and water', the latter being the water. On more mature consideration, Queen Sophie was forced to agree with Queen Victoria's view: 'poor Princess Mary! I see no chances of her marrying in Germany. She gaspilléd her life forlornly.' Evidently the Dutch queen blamed the Duchess of Cambridge feeling that the latter ought to have played her cards better when the princess was younger and less of a problem both in size and manner. It was clear to any observer that the Cambridge family's annual campaigns in Germany were 'as fruitless for Princess Mary as all the preceding ones'. Yet despite the lack of success the Duke of Cambridge remained optimistic, observing that 'some Younger Brother who need not be always in Germany and whom it might suit him [sic] to live occasionally in England would be the best husband'. But where was such a paragon and if he existed would he be prepared to marry a very stout princess who was now definitely regarded as an old maid?

A couple of more years elapsed; but despite the Duke of Cambridge's Micawberish hopes that something would turn up, nothing did. Another brother of Edward of Saxe-Weimar was considered but he was soon rejected as being 'dull, borne

Prince (later Duke) Francis of Teck at the time of his marriage.
(From The Illustrated London News)

H.I.M. Elizabeth, Empress of Austria, was one of the most beautiful women of her day. In contrast to Princess Mary the Empress was very slender. She dieted and exercised constantly to keep herself slim. The Empress and her husband were very fond of the Duke of Teck and had supervised his early education.
(From a private collection)

and obstinate and full of *morgue*' the last being 'German prince's *morgue* which is like no other'. In addition, Queen Sophie of the Netherlands characterized him as 'stupid, speaks no English, and hardly any French' and she thought if Princess Mary married such a fool the marriage would be impossible.

The sorry tale continued with the Prussians trotting out a dreary widower, the Duke of Mecklenburg-Schwerin, or his less interesting – if that be possible – brother William. However, the Grand Duke was dominated by his mother who only wished for a nice quiet princess whom she could control and was totally opposed to the idea of her son marrying the strong-minded and independent Princess Mary. The other Mecklenburg prince was known to be wildly extravagant and had been refused by a number of princesses already. Clearly neither of these candidates was likely to win much approbation. The impoverished Prince Waldemar of Holstein had a couple of assets; he was so poor he would have to live in England with his wife's family and seemed prepared to disregard Lord Clarendon's gloomy dictum 'that no German prince will venture on *so vast an undertaking*'. He, too, was unsuitable. The Queen in despair and agreeing with Clarendon's gloom wrote to her daughter, 'Poor Mary. Is there no chance at all?' From all appearances the prospects were inauspicious.

Princess Mary now made it clear that life at a small German court was totally abhorrent to her. Having been rejected by so many minor princelings she took the stance of rejecting all that they embodied. She was resigned to being her mother's companion but pleased only to be able to live in England which she adored. It seemed as if Princess Mary was doomed to be the perpetual spinster, a figure so much in evidence in the novels of Victorian life. However, Princess Mary's fairy godmother had not abandoned her totally. Rescue was in sight and a Prince Charming of sorts was about to enter her life.

The prince in question was Francis of Teck and he was discovered by Albert Edward, Prince of Wales, who met him in Vienna and took an instant liking to him. Prince Francis of Teck was the son of Duke Alexander of Württemberg, who had married a Countess Rhedey; the lady was very beautiful and, as Queen Sophie of the Netherlands noted, 'virtuous and good'. However, because the countess was not of equal birth to her husband, the marriage, while legitimate, was morganatic. By making such a marriage Duke Alexander forfeited his rights of succession to the Württemberg crown. From her comments on various occasions it would appear that Queen Victoria thought the whole business of morganatic marriages an absurdity – in any case such a thing does not exist in England as a woman takes her husband's rank if his is superior to her own – and always felt it wrong that the Tecks could not become the sovereigns of Württemberg any more than the Battenbergs could not succeed in Hesse.

Because of the emphasis placed on equal birth, *ebenbürtig*, there was only a rather limited number of choices for individuals of royal rank and by the nineteenth century they were all more or less related. The problem was compounded by the division of protestant and Roman Catholic families and they only rarely crossed lines. Some families such as the House of Hohenzollern, for example, had protestant and Roman Catholic branches as did the Württembergers. The Saxe-Coburgs, who were very opportunistic, seemed very willing to marry to promote their interests even if it meant possible religious differences. For example, Leopold I of Belgium's second wife was a daughter of King Louis-Philippe and their children were Roman Catholic while he remained a Protestant. When he died there were a number of complications about his funeral. Although superficially there appeared to be a plethora of families, such was not the case and, because of their close relationships, hereditary diseases such as haemophilia were passed about within the royal houses to a far greater degree than among the population generally. Prince Albert had been much worried about the situation, as was his wife later to become. Writing to her eldest daughter she said, 'I do *wish* one could find some more black eyed Pces or Pcesses... I can't help thinking what dear Papa said – that it was in fact a blessing when there was some little *imperfection* in the *pure Royal* descent and that some fresh blood was infused... constant fair hair and blue eyes makes the blood so lymphatic,' and she concluded by observing that the Prince Consort had on more than one occasion said firmly, '*We must have some strong dark blood.*' Theoretically, there had been some potential 'strong dark blood' added to the royal marriage market with the new ruling families that came into being as a result of the Napoleonic empire. For example, the Bonapartes were not related to many of the reigning families: indeed they were scarcely regarded as royal, nor were the Bernadottes in Sweden nor, for that matter, were the Leuchtenburgs, or the Murats. Some of Napoleon's marshals had been made princes and they were probably the equal in birth to the mediatized families – former sovereign princes prior to the dissolution of the Holy Roman Empire – but since the majority of the former military officers were Roman Catholics they did little for protestant families. In any case at best they were merely thought to have been ennobled and not much more. This would certainly not bring them into the circle.

Those with 'little imperfection in the pure Royal descent' were very conscious of their position. Indeed the 'imperfections' made them more and more insistent upon their supposed or hoped-for rights. Queen Sophie of the Netherlands, who was a very liberal minded individual, commenting on the problem, said of another (and in this instance a 'perfect royal') as being 'one of those who cannot bear the second place... I always wonder when clever people dwindle away their lives with such petty preoccupations.' Such sentiments were easy enough to express when one was secure. The 'imperfect royals' were constantly on the *qui vive* to promote themselves; every privilege given by reigning house became another triumph; each rejection a matter for deep despair. The questions of precedence and the like may seem trivial but it was deemed a matter of the utmost importance if one went into the 'closet' with the royal family, or if one were received at the head or the foot of the stairs upon arrival, or if one had a full guard of honour and a band at a railway station, or if one were accorded apartments in a palace or could avail oneself of the royal yacht. Moreover in Germany in particular the gradations between serene highness, highness, royal highness and imperial highness were strictly enforced. In England the problem did not arise. Either one was legitimate and with full rank or one was illegitimate and a commoner. Because morganatic marriages were unknown to English law the offspring of all legal marriages were legitimate. For example, the son and daughter of Prince William, Duke of Gloucester and brother of King George III, were 'royal highness' even though their mother did not have royal birth because the marriage was legal. On the other hand the three sons of Prince George, Duke of Cambridge, were not royal highnesses because the duke's marriage was not in conformity with the law. Technically, the three Fitzgeorges were illegitimate even though their father always regarded their mother as his wife. Indeed, the whole complicated business was another manifestation of the rigid social conventions of the nineteenth century.

Despite the lack of *ebenbürtig* rank, Duke Alexander and his wife were very happy and three children were born of the marriage, a son and two daughters. Unfortunately the Countess Hohenstein, Duke Alexander's wife, was killed in a rather bizarre accident in 1841. She was on horseback at a military review in Vienna; somehow her horse became frightened, ran away with her, and she was thrown to the ground. At that precise moment a troop of cavalry were passing at full gallop and she was trampled to death. Everyone was vastly sorry for Duke Alexander and his children and they became the subject of interest and concern.

In particular Duke Alexander's son found very influential patrons in the Austrian Emperor and his wife. They grew to like the lad, described by one relation as 'a beautiful boy', and continued their interest in him as he grew older. Count Hohenstein, as he was called, joined the Austrian army serv-

H.S.H. Prince Francis of Teck at the time of his marriage. From this picture it is quite clear why he was known in Vienna as 'der schöne Uhlan'.
(From the collection of H.M. The Queen)

ing as an officer in the Imperial Gendarmerie Guard. In 1859 he was at the Battle of Solferino where he gained the reputation of being a good soldier. He was charming and good looking, known in Vienna as 'der Schöne Uhlan'. The Austrians persuaded the King of Württemberg to raise his rank and he became a Serene Highness and Prince of Teck. He would have preferred to be called a Prince of Württemberg or Prince Württemberg like the Prussian Prince Hohenzollern but this King Frederick of Württemberg was disinclined to do. His prospects were somewhat improved but he was not rich. His cousin Queen Sophie characterized him as 'very handsome, as poor as Job without any position' and without even a house; however, he was 'good natured and good tempered'. He had a number of admirers including the Princess Catherine of Württemberg, who had a secret passion for him and hoped to become his wife. His lack of wealth and his uncertain social position did not make him an eligible *parti* to her family, however.

To show his approbation of Prince Teck, the Prince of Wales proposed that he come to England. Teck arrived in the autumn of 1865 and very quickly he established himself as a social success. His Viennese charm, his affability and his handsome appearance ensured him a favourable reception with all the hostesses in London. Moreover while there is no proof it is possible that the Prince of Wales had thought of him as a solution to the question of a husband for Princess Mary. It is clear that the Cambridge family did not take the initiative but had the idea put to them by the Prince of Wales among others. They recognized the fact that he had no money and Princess Mary herself was not rich but her family hoped that with good management and some financial assistance they would be all right as a couple.

Princess Mary's mother, brother and sister decided to be very cautious. There had been too many difficulties and sorrows with other prospective suitors. They all felt that marriage would settle her down as she had been spoilt by everyone, being the youngest and still single. They believed that once ensconced in a cosy and happy domestic situation she would be less extravagant – this was to be a pious hope indeed – and as Queen Mary was later to say, 'Everyone seemed to think it would do – and it did.'

While all the royal matchmakers were hard at work, Princess Mary was at Strelitz where for once she seems to have pleased everyone. This meant that all of her family were actively in support of what her sister said 'our last chance'. Rather than risk a meeting until matters were relatively settled the family kept her in ignorance of what was occurring in London. When things seemed likely to be successful the Duchess of Cambridge, who had not spent the winter at Strelitz as she so often did, sent for her daughter saying that her company was essential. Upon receipt of the letter from London the Grand Duchess of Mecklenburg-Strelitz packed her sister off accompanied by Frau Willicken Schieve a woman who might have modelled for Miss Prism as described by Lady Bracknell, that is 'of repellent aspect', but loyal and trustworthy. In any case, she would be unobtrusive at such a crucial time. With the return of the princess all that now mattered was for Prince Francis' arrival and a formal proposal. The prince had arranged to reach England in mid-March, and less than a month after he had landed, he and Princess Mary were formally engaged. Her mother wrote, 'I am happy to say I feel sure of dear Mary's future happiness. Prince Teck seems to be a most excellent young man, good principled, most religious, perfect manners – in short, I call Mary a most fortunate creature to have found such a husband.' The princess herself was ecstatic: 'How happy I am and with what confiding hope I can (D.V.) look forward to a future of bright promise as he is... all *I* could wish...' Her more realistic sister, Augusta, observed to her brother, the Duke of Cambridge, 'We can wish *her* and *ourselves* joy that this marriage has been settled.... We can but be happy and grateful for this *wonderful* and happy *conclusion.*'

Immediately all of the family far and near were informed. Prince Francis' cousin, the Queen of the Netherlands, was a

H.M. King Charles I of Württemberg, half-brother of Queen Sophie of the Netherlands. King Charles and his wife were childless and if the Duke of Teck had not been the issue of a morganatic marriage he would have succeeded King Charles in Württemberg.
(From an anonymous watercolour on paper in the collection of H.M. Queen Beatrix of the Netherlands)

little surprised that the Duchess was so pleased with her prospective son-in-law since she was so very proud of her rank and position and 'il n'y a pas de quoi'. Rank and position he may not have had nor money either but he was ready to marry a princess who was not young and who was for her day regarded as an old maid. He was also prepared to live in England which was a further dividend. Queen Victoria initially had some misgivings about Prince Francis chiefly because he was a friend of her eldest son. She rather disapproved of what she called 'that set'. But once the engagement was determined she was pleased that her cousin's future was settled. Prince Francis was asked to Osborne to be inspected and the Queen's verdict was 'very nice and amiable, thoroughly unassuming and very gentlemanlike and certainly very good looking'. Because the Cambridge family were so well known to society and to the public generally, great interest was shown in the engagement. Numerous copies of the *carte de visite* photograph of Prince Francis were on display everywhere and in particular in London where Princess Mary was a popular personality.

While preparations for the marriage were taking place, the purchasing of the trousseau, the making of the bridal gown and the sending of the invitations, the family also occupied themselves with the problems of Teck's rank. They would have liked him to be created a Duke of Württemberg but it was evident King Charles of Württemberg was not favourably disposed to confer such a title. Indeed, Prince Francis' cousin, the Queen of the Netherlands, put the matter more succinctly; the anti-Teck sentiment came not exclusively from King Charles but also from his wife, Queen Olga, the daughter of Tsar Nicholas of Russia. The Dutch Queen was of the opinion that as long as Queen Olga had any influence there would be no better title for Teck. The former was disinclined to enhance the latter's position because somehow it might make him and others believe he had some rights of succession to the throne of Württemberg. Queen Victoria would not give him the rank of 'Highness' either but she did

Princess Mary at the time of her marriage.
(From The Illustrated London News)

give him the Order of the Bath as a sign of his acceptance into the family. The Cambridge family were tireless in their efforts but all were unavailing. Francis of Teck remained as he was and they had to be content. Even later Princess Mary was to try and get special privileges writing at one time to persuade the House of Orange to declare that as a collateral of that family he ought not to pay taxes. The Dutch monarchs thought it all very silly and declined to support such a request. Prince Francis did ultimately get his dukedom from Württemberg; in 1871 he was created Duke of Teck, but the question of his rank remained unchanged and it was to be a sore point in the years to come. However, in 1887 on the occasion of her Golden Jubilee Queen Victoria gave him the personal rank of 'Highness' much to his pleasure and that of his wife. Nevertheless, their children still bore the rank of serene highness much to the continued chagrin of their parents.

The dressmakers were hard put to get everything ready for the 12th June. It was emphasized that British materials alone should be bought and local people in Kew were used as much as possible to supply the materials. The *Illustrated London News* described the bridal gown:

> the dress was composed of white satin and tulle, and trimmed with three flounces of Honiton lace. The train was likewise of white satin with similar flounces of lace and it was secured to the dress by bouquets of orange-flowers and myrtle.... The head-dress consisted of a wreath of orange-blossoms, inter-mixed with myrtle gathered in Kew Gardens, and surmounted at the back with a diamond flower.

The bridesmaids wore blue, the favourite colour of the bride.

Sensibly the Duchess of Cambridge decided that the whole affair would be as simple as possible. While there were to be the usual contingent of royal and distinguished guests the Cambridges desired to include, as far as was feasible, all of

The Bridal procession leaving the Kew Church after the marriage of Princess Mary and Francis of Teck. The bride and groom are followed by the Duke of Cambridge and Queen Victoria. (From The Illustrated London News)

The departure of Princess Mary and the Prince of Teck from Kew after their marriage.
(From The Illustrated London News)

Kew and in this they were remarkably successful. Local people were to sit in the parish church with their sovereign and all as guests of the family. This was not an affair of state and was devoid of the usual pomp. The widowed Queen, accompanied by her two daughters, Helena and Louise, took their places in chairs near the altar while the other royal personages such as the Duchess of Cambridge, the Prince and Princess of Wales, the Grand Duke and Grand Duchess of Mecklenburg-Strelitz, and the Duke of Edinburgh made a formal procession into the little church with the women in day clothes and the men in civilian dress without decorations being worn. The bride was given away by her brother and there was a family wedding breakfast at Cambridge Cottage. Late in the afternoon the bridal couple drove off to Ashridge for the honeymoon.

Alas! the pleasure of the whole affair was blighted by events in Germany. As the guests were dressing for the ceremony, telegrams were on their way recounting what was happening in Frankfurt. Austria and Prussia had come to the parting of the ways over Schleswig and Holstein and war was inevitable. The petty German states had to choose sides. The two Mecklenburgs and Oldenburg had little choice but to join Prussia, who quickly occupied Hanover, Saxony and Hesse and plans were put into operation for an invasion of Austrian territory. Francis of Teck as a serving officer in Francis Joseph's army felt he must immediately return to Vienna, and to take up such duties as might be required of him.

After only a fortnight at Ashridge, the Tecks left England and initially made their way to Württemberg, where Princess Mary was to remain while her husband betook himself to Austria. Princess Mary, who had a horror of small German courts with their rigid etiquette and formality, went to Ludwigsburg, where she was a guest of the Queen Dowager. Her stay was not a happy one partly because of the deteriorating military situation for the anti-Prussian forces and partly because of the stifling atmosphere of the society. Prince Francis did not reach the imperial capital until after the Austrians had been defeated at Königrätz and so confused were affairs in Vienna that he was kept waiting about with no instructions or orders. Following a week of frustration, he left and returned to his bride and the two of them proceeded to Vienna together to wait upon events. Her sister, the Grand Duchess of Mecklenburg-Strelitz, was convinced that they would ultimately go to Budapest because she thought the Prussians would continue to march directly to Vienna. They took up residence at the Hotel Münsch and after spending something more than a month in idleness Prince Francis was finally given something to do just before the armistice was signed.

Apparently his duties were hardly onerous because they settled at Liesing about an hour's drive from Vienna and very shortly were joined by Prince Francis's two sisters. His father Duke Alexander was already in residence and they had an agreeable family gathering. However, they were all much saddened by the fact that Hanover, Electoral Hesse and Nassau were now only Prussian provinces and that the ruling families, their own near relations, were in exile.

By mid-October the worst was over. The victors had determined the future of Germany and Prince Francis was released from his military duties. Indeed, this was to be the end of his career in the Austrian army; he hoped, of course, for a similar posting in England but such was not to be, though he was not to know this in 1866. Indeed, all he ever became was the Honorary Colonel of the City of London Post Office Volunteers seeing brief active service in Egypt in 1882.

Before resuming life in England, where it was obviously understood that the Tecks would make their base near Princess Mary's family, they paid a visit to Princess Amelia, who had married a Count von Hügel. The von Hügels lived in Schloss Reinthal which was situated near Graz in Styria. The Schloss was not new having initially been built in the sixteenth century, nor was it overly large and was not very grand; indeed, it was much in the style of Rumpenheim being built around three sides of a square. The gardens were attractive and the views appealing. Everyone agreed that Styrian countryside was agreeable at all times of the year. Reinthal was not the residence of a great family but more the home of civilized people with simple and uncomplicated lives and after the unpleasant events of the summer, both Francis of Teck and his wife felt very comfortable and at their ease in such a pleasant rural retreat. Another nice feature of the Reinthal was that they could also enjoy the company of Princess Claudine, their other sister, who had built a little house in the style of a Swiss chalet on the grounds of the estate. The von Hügels, the Tecks and their unmarried sister could easily foregather every evening and not only discuss happier days in the past, but regard with concern the future of their dispossessed relations now 'exiled and homeless'.

By mid-November it was necessary for a move to be made and the homeward journey to be undertaken. A series of brief visits to Stuttgart, Rumpenheim, Brussels and Paris were on the itinerary. Paris was the occasion for a sitting by Princess Mary to Franz Winterhalter, that ubiquitous portrayer of royalty in the nineteenth century. His pictures were all agreeably idealized, the general likeness softened and improved – and his painting of Princess Mary was no exception. This was the second occasion that the princess had been the subject of a picture by Winterhalter and once again she and her family were delighted with his work.

The Channel crossing in December was dreadfully uncomfortable but after their six months abroad they were vastly pleased to be settled at Kew as guests of the Duchess of Cambridge. Their permanent home was to be in Kensington Palace; they were to have the same rooms formerly occupied by Queen Victoria and her mother. As Princess Mary noted, however, some improvements were needed and if the Board of Works were willing 'to spend a little money' their apartments could 'be made a very charming abode, as the rooms are handsome and comfortable'.

Prince Francis, who had no settled occupation, busied himself with selecting the wallpaper and furnishings for his new home. His wife encouraged him in his activities as she recognized that he had a real flair and excellent taste. 'He had,' it was observed, 'the art of making his surroundings thoroughly comfortable.' Indeed, interior decoration, collecting Chinese porcelain and gardening were to be his principal activities for the remainder of his life. It was not particularly an existence he would have chosen for himself. He always hoped for a renewed career in the army or in some public capacity but this was not to be. He had to be content with the position of merely being the husband of Princess Mary and later as the paterfamilias of their children.

The relations were not entirely sure how well the new establishment would succeed. However, he quickly showed that at home he was master. Queen Victoria noted that he had 'a vy firm will and opinion of his own' but Queen Sophie feared for the future as he was known to be 'a passionate admirer of thin, pale beauties' and his wife certainly did not fall into this category. As the years passed there was to be the occasional gossip; the Duchess of Hamilton reported hearing that he had run off to Rome with another woman but there was no truth in the story. His cousin, the Queen of the Netherlands, noted that he was 'natural' and 'sensible' and 'not afraid of being too *little* valued in rank' and that he could accept 'his whole position with good sense and good judgement'. Nevertheless, it cannot have been easy and Prince Francis was occasionally irascible, often irritable and somewhat restless. However, early in his marriage he was buoyed up by love for his wife and later for their children and in the hopes that, as with the Micawbers, 'something would turn up', to provide an occupation that would utilize his talents.

There was some urgency in the Teck household regarding the projected move to Kensington Palace as Princess Mary was pregnant. They were scarcely settled in their new abode when the baby arrived; it was a daughter, born on 26th May, 1867. As with royal accouchements, there were the usual gaggle of attendants and female relations and official representatives. There had been much concern for the health of the princess and the prospect of her first child because she was

The Morning Room at Kensington Palace. Note the many portraits of relations and fancy furnishings. Through the archway the Tecks' bed is to be seen.
(From the collection of H.M. The Queen)

aged thirty-four. Yet all went well. Her sister Augusta of Mecklenburg-Strelitz was on hand, arriving uncharacteristically in advance of the event, and the good news was immediately sent to the Duchess of Cambridge at Kew and to Queen Victoria at Balmoral. Visitors arrived 'to sign the book' to express their felicitations and over a thousand names were to be recorded. Perhaps Queen Victoria summed up the general sentiments of everyone in Britain: 'I need not repeat to you, my dearest Mary, how *truly*, really happy I have been at your safe and prosperous confinement and the birth of your little girl. I have known you and loved you dearly from your earliest *infancy*... and your happiness has ever been near my heart – and therefore my joy at this event is *most sincere*.'

The newly born infant was given a long list of names. Initially Agnes was to be her Christian name in memory of Prince Francis' grandmother but the Cambridge family decreed that Victoria was more suitable, and they were to prevail, but the princess was soon to be called 'May' by all of her relations and this is how the public knew her. A month after the infant's birth, she was christened Victoria Mary Augusta Louisa Olga Pauline Claudine Agnes – note the fact that Teck names now trailed at the end – with the Queen as one of her godmothers, the other two being her grandmother and her Aunt Augusta.

To almost universal astonishment, Princess Mary was soon once more on the social scene. She and her husband were part of the royal assembly to welcome the Sultan of Turkey and the Viceroy of Egypt. So busy was she that she had to observe 'there is something going on morning noon and night and my poor head is quite confused with all the bustle and excitement' but she would not have missed it for she vastly enjoyed the applause of the crowd. Her cousin, the Crown Princess of Prussia, was to remark, 'Mary is very popular, and justly so,' but she added somewhat caustically, 'Still I think she courts popularity'. And this she did because she was sincerely fond of everyone and expected her enthusiasm to be reciprocated.

The Tecks like other members of society left the capital at the end of the season and made a round of country house visits and then took a short tour of the continent. They visited the Paris Exposition which they vastly enjoyed. A number of their relations were also to come to the French capital for this last grand occasion of the Second Empire. Only Francis Joseph was to withdraw his acceptance but this was because his brother Maximilian had been executed in Mexico. It was all the more difficult since the Habsburg prince was a French protegé. Another royal visitor found Paris much to his liking and this was King William of Prussia; the next time he came to the French capital it was under very different circumstances, namely as conqueror rather than a guest and with his former host as his prisoner.

Rumpenheim and Stuttgart were both in the Teck itinerary; and a continental sojourn with friends and relations was much to their liking. However, with parliament due to resume sitting the season would begin anew, and, therefore, they hastened back to Kensington Palace to enjoy the London social scene.

Although Queen Victoria had called to see her cousin in June, the Tecks had not been her guests at Windsor. In mid-November, they were summoned for a night; it was initially the plan that the infant princess would come too but she had a cold and was left at home. Two weeks later the whole family arrived; Queen Victoria was delighted to see them all so happy but she noted, 'It is a *real* pleasure to see dear Mary.... But her *size* is fearful! It is *really* a misfortune' and observed 'She is alas! grown enormous.'

The family spent Christmas at Kensington Palace and then went off to Cambridge Cottage for the New Year. It was all very *gemütlich*. The Duchess of Cambridge busied herself with knitting, Princess Mary looked at albums and placed photographs in proper books, and Prince Francis played duets with Lord Frederick Paulet. Certainly no one would be able to say that the Tecks lived in a 'fast' manner.

Princess Mary was pregnant once again but this did not

seem to diminish her activities. There was the usual making of visits to friends which were only curtailed shortly before the birth of a son on 13th August 1868. The boy was christened Adolphus after his grandfather and cousin. Throughout his life he was called 'Dolly' by the family and friends. A second son, Francis, followed some eighteen months later; he was born on 9th January 1870. This boy was known as Frank. The family was completed with a third son four years later, Prince Alexander, who was born on 14th April 1874. His family nickname was 'Alge' – coming from his two names Alexander and George.

As before and again to everyone's amazement, Princess Mary was soon up and about after Prince Dolly's birth and two months later she was delighted to accept an invitation from Queen Victoria to visit Balmoral. Princess Mary had never visited the Queen's Deeside home before and recognized that it was a signal honour to have been asked to stay. Queen Victoria at this stage in her life was still in mourning for the Prince Consort, and, moreover, Balmoral was so much associated with the happy days of the past; outsiders were somewhat of an intrusion. The journey to the Queen's highland home must have seemed endless. Departing in the early evening from London the Tecks arrived in Scotland by mid-morning. Apparently the sleeping arrangements on the train provided were not very comfortable but of course the Princess's size might have been part of the difficulty. The route north took them from Euston via Edinburgh to Perth where they breakfasted, then on to Aberdeen and finally 'a special' to Ballater. Like Queen Victoria and Prince Albert, the Tecks made comparisons between the Highlands and romantic scenery elsewhere, in the former case it was with Coburg, in the latter with Transylvania.

Upon arrival at Balmoral – and orders had been given that the Tecks were to reach the castle after it was dark – they were greeted with the highland servants holding lighted torches, the pipers were present with a welcoming tune, and the Queen and her family at the door. The local people danced a

The Council Room at Kensington Palace used by the Tecks as a sitting-room. The picture was taken in the Summer because the furniture is covered with bright cheerful material and the fireplace has a fan in front of it.
(From the collection of H.M. The Queen)

Balmoral Castle, circa 1865, as it would have looked about the time Princess Mary and the Duke (then Prince) of Teck were guests of Queen Victoria.
(Photograph by G. Wilson)

reel in honour of the guests and then put their torches together for a bonfire. The Tecks were enchanted; the highlands once more worked their magic on the visitor. No doubt the ghillies were not unhappy either as such occasions meant 'a dram all round!'

Everything pleased, the rooms were described as 'charming' with the carpets of Royal Stuart tartan, curtains of Dress Stuart or Victoria, the furniture made of natural wood, and, as decorations, numerous mounted stags' heads, many of which were trophies of the late Prince Consort, basket swords, sporrans and claymores on the wall. There were drives to various beauty spots, meals *al fresco* with the inevitable roast potatoes and although it rained everyone was in the best of humour; there was tea with the wives of the estate workers and the inevitable ghillies' ball. A perfect holiday as the mid-Victorians would have imagined it. The week at Balmoral passed all too quickly – nobody seems to have made very extended sojourns with Queen Victoria except her younger children – and the Tecks returned to London for the season. 'As a souvenir of dear Scotland' the Queen wrote '[I send] [a] Hunting Stewart velvet dress... wh. I hope will be acceptable.' The Tecks were not again to visit Balmoral for over twenty years until Princess May, their daughter, was under serious consideration as a bride for the Duke of Clarence and Avondale.

Queen Victoria had generously allowed the Tecks a quite extensive suite in Kensington Palace. The entrance was from Clock Court and a visitor would pass through a hall into what was called The Council Room, so named because Queen Victoria's Accession Council had been held there, which served to receive guests. Leading from this reception room was the saloon. To the right of the latter was the Blue Drawing Room and to the left a large dining room. There was also a sitting room for Prince Francis, a boudoir for his wife – this also served as a morning room – as well as bedrooms, dressing rooms and nurseries. The whole had been put into order by the Department of Works and Prince Francis had ensured that the general decoration and furnishings were suitable. There was also a private garden in which the Tecks would take tea in the summer.

Despite their lack of wealth Princess Mary and her husband lived in a manner of some style. There was always a retinue of servants to ensure that the royal couple and their children were comfortable. However, it was never to be quite good enough, for the Tecks were ever anxious to promote their position. Their servants were in a livery very little different to that of the Queen much to the annoyance of the latter. She pointedly noted some years later, 'This should not be!' and that 'Livery or undress should be their own'. Her disapproval seems to have had little effect and to the casual observer the livery worn by Princess Mary's servants was identical to that of the sovereign and the carriages were 'exactly the same as the Queen's with the exception of the difference of the Crowns'. The Duke of Teck might only be a Serene Highness in the royal precedence game but only the most perceptive would be able to discern that the establishment differed in any way from his wife's and other grander connections. They were exceedingly hospitable and their invitations to dine were enthusiastically accepted. The food and drink were of the best quality, the flowers and fruits were the freshest, and the first of the season, and the servants well trained. Princess Mary resplendent in yards of velvet and lace and wearing the jewels left to her by the Duchess of Gloucester was in her element as a hostess while Prince Francis in full evening dress with medals and the red ribbon of the Bath across his chest was elegant, charming and handsome. The best of London society mingled happily and Kensington Palace had few rivals.

All of this was expensive but the cost never seemed to be considered. Money was not a subject in polite conversation and tradesmen would never dunn their royal patrons. The former were, however, rewarded by the latter by being allowed the designation 'Purveyors to Her Royal Highness the Princess Mary Adelaide, Duchess of Teck' which in those

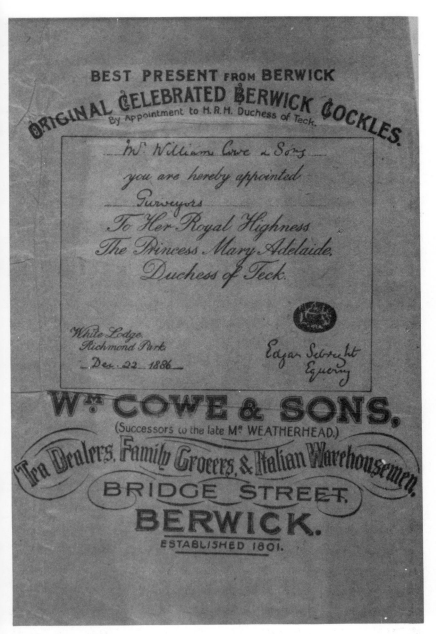

BEST PRESENT FROM BERWICK

ORIGINAL CELEBRATED BERWICK COCKLES.

By Appointment to H.R.H. Duchess of Teck.

Mr William Cowe & Sons

you are hereby appointed

Surveyors

To Her Royal Highness
The Princess Mary Adelaide,
Duchess of Teck.

White Lodge,
Richmond Park.
Dec. 22 1886

Edgar Sebright
Equerry

W^M COWE & SONS,
(Successors to the late Mr WEATHERHEAD.)

Tea Dealers, Family Grocers, & Italian Warehousemen.

BRIDGE STREET,

BERWICK.

ESTABLISHED 1801.

One of those fashionable and snobbish aspects of Victorian life — royal patronage to shopkeepers attracted middle-class people to their shops.
(From a private collection)

days meant a great deal to a tradesman and was a consolation for unpaid bills. Moreover, friends, kind friends, were extremely understanding and their generosity ensured that Princess Mary could continue to enjoy herself. Angela Burdett-Coutts was particularly helpful in emergencies, and consequently the overdraft was reduced a bit but very quickly it mounted up anew. Princess Mary never understood money and was quite determined to remain ignorant. Knowledge would be unpleasant and she declined to face reality on these matters. Indeed, it is apparent that even if she had the income of the Tsar of Russia she would always overspend. Money was only to get you what you wanted and the lack of it was at worst an inconvenience, not a barrier to living as one thought right.

One thing was lacking and that was 'a place', that is, a country house. Everyone who was anybody had such an establishment. The Queen had Balmoral and Osborne as well as Windsor; the Prince of Wales had Sandringham and all of the Tecks' friends had residences outside London, the Scarboroughs 'a place' at Sandbeck, Lady Marion Alford at Ashbridge, the Derbys at Knowsley and the like. Moreover, all of their continental relations had rural retreats: at Hanover, Princess Mary as a child had spent the summer at Monbrilliant, an attractive country house belonging to the Electors of Hanover, and country *Schlosser* dotted the German landscape.

A possible solution might be found in 'a grace and favour' house. To be sure it was unlikely that the Queen would welcome the Tecks at Balmoral and on the highland estate nothing was available, nor for that matter was there anything suitable at Osborne. Indeed, neither the Isle of Wight nor Scotland were quite what the Tecks envisaged; they wanted something convenient enough to London but at the same time a house that would qualify as 'a place'. Certainly apartments in Hampton Court would hardly suit; there was nothing at Kew; Frogmore would not have been considered – it was still a sort of shrine to Queen Victoria's mother and also part of the whole cult of the Prince Consort. York Cottage was not in good repair, and Bushey was really almost suburban. One highly desirable house remained and that was White Lodge in Richmond. To add to its attraction it had close family connections with Princess Mary having been the country retreat of her beloved Aunt Mary.

White Lodge was an early Georgian building which had been made into a commodious house over the years. Queen Caroline, the wife of George II, had been particularly attracted to the place and had used it frequently. George III's political ally the Marquess of Bute was Ranger of Richmond Park and he had lived in White Lodge from time to time. Later Lord Sidmouth had been given life tenancy and upon his death it had been granted to the Duchess of Gloucester when she succeeded her father to the post Bute had held earlier. After 1857 it reverted to the Crown once more, and Queen Victoria occupied it occasionally. In 1858 the Prince of Wales and his tutors lived there. One wing was fitted up at that time for his use and remained known thereafter as 'The Prince of Wales Wing'; following the demise of the Duchess of Kent in the spring of 1861 the Queen herself resided in it for a short time. A wing comprising six rooms was hastily refurbished and it was called 'The Queen's Wing'. After she ceased to use it, White Lodge was lent for a time to Lady Phipps; in the years 1867 and 1868 the Wales's made some use of it but they preferred Chiswick House when they wanted to escape from London for a short time.

Princess Mary came to the conclusion that White Lodge would be most satisfactory and began a campaign to persuade her cousin to let her have it. Queen Victoria was not overly enthusiastic but finally agreed to allow the Tecks to occupy it for a month in 1869. Their stay convinced them that White Lodge was exactly what they required. Princess Mary used all of her wiles to convince the Queen to agree to the Teck family becoming the permanent residents. Victoria took considerable persuading, fond as she was of Princess Mary. After much hesitation and despite her misgivings she finally agreed.

The library at White Lodge, Windsor, was a favourite room of the Duke of Teck. Notice the sofa covered with a leopard skin and the East Africa table. Both very fashionable in Victorian interiors.
(From the collection of H.M. The Queen)

The Green Corridor at White Lodge, Windsor was used by the Tecks as a sort of sitting room. The furniture and pictures were arranged by the Duke who had a great interest in interior decoration.
(From the collection of H.M. The Queen)

128

Once permission was granted the Tecks lost no time in taking possession. Of course the suite of apartments at Kensington Palace was not formally abandoned and served as a London headquarters, being always kept ready for use if required. However, White Lodge was now to be 'home' for the Tecks until their death. A year after she took up residence, Princess Mary observed, 'We have been leading a very quiet pleasant life in this our country home, which we are quite devoted to'. These sentiments would serve to express her own and her family's feelings for the future.

White Lodge is an uncomplicated building of a central block with two wings and connecting corridors. One of the latter was called 'The childrens' corridor' leading to 'the Queen's Wing' and the other 'the Green Corridor' leading to 'the Prince of Wales Wing'. The house had a handsome sitting room, drawing room and dining room, a library and in addition a number of small rooms for more intimate living. Indeed, many of the bedrooms were quite pokey and not entirely satisfactory. There were some furnishings but many new pieces were acquired from Maples at no inconsiderable cost and the whole was almost the *beau-idéal* of Victorian decor. As in the past Prince Francis took charge of the interior decoration with every inch of wall covered with pictures and tables and whatnots everywhere. Much of his time was passed over the years in re-ordering the furniture and pictures as he had little else to do. He also took up gardening with avidity and with excellent results and the five acres of grounds were vastly improved. White Lodge soon took on a cosy domestic feeling both inside and outside.

Since White Lodge was so conveniently located, the Tecks were able to enjoy the social life which had given them so much pleasure in London. Friends could easily drive out from the city to see them: it was only ten miles from Kensington, and it was not very distant from Cambridge Cottage which meant that Princess Mary could make a daily call on her mother. It was also handy to Windsor if the Queen required the company of her cousin and her husband.

Life at White Lodge seems to have been extraordinarily simple much of the time. Princess Mary's journal tells of calls by her friends and their children, teas on the lawn, duets on the piano in the evening with Prince Francis, primroses gathered in the woods, games with her own children – always referred to by their mamma as 'the chicks' – and the occasional dinner party. It was in so many ways not very different from many upper-class households of the day. While the Tecks never forgot their special position as members of the royal family, at the same time they were astonishingly informal and *gemütlich*. A guest observed, 'It was a pretty sight to see the Royal parents with their young family at tea-time under the old apple tree in the garden'. Family events were the highlights of the year, birthdays and Christmas in particular.

At Christmas, for example, there were trees for the servants with presents for them all as well as a special dinner. For the family there was a large tree in the drawing room with gifts on tables, a separate one for each person. Presents had arrived from all of the relations in the continent and from the Queen and her children; moreover, since the Tecks had a wide circle of friends the latter gave generously as well. Over the holiday season Princess Mary and her husband made visits to Windsor, to St James's Palace and to Marlborough House. At the festive season there were grand dinners with numerous courses – the Tecks were great eaters as were many of their contemporaries – and meals went on for hours. There seem to have been unending rich casseroles, roasts, lobster salad and fruit with cream. It is hardly surprising, therefore, that neither Princess Mary nor the Prince of Wales, both of whom were good trenchermen, ever lost weight despite the fact that medical science was already aware that obesity was dangerous. Nevertheless, dieting was inconceivable, and, besides, to be thin had not yet become fashionable. To be sure, the Princess of Wales who was very slender was much admired but in general the taste ran to what was called 'a fine figure of a woman', one of ten stone at least, and the Duchess of Teck while stout was not thought to be unwomanly.

While domesticity and society absorbed much of the life of
Princess Mary, there was a third element to which she gave
much attention and to which she was to devote more and
more time as the years passed. Charitable activities of various
sorts were to be of great concern to her and she was to work
very hard for those organizations with which she became
involved. She was not content merely to be the patroness
alone but she was a full working member of the committee.
While incompetent in managing her own finances she was
extremely adept in keeping her charities solvent. An early
charitable body to which she was particularly committed, as
indeed were her mother and brother and to a lesser extent of
her sister in Germany, was the Royal Cambridge Asylum.

This institution had been founded by the Duchess of Cambridge and her sister-in-law, the Duchess of Gloucester, in
memory of Princess Mary's father. It was to house seventy
soldiers' widows and each had a modest allowance of five
shillings a week; they were given a room, furnishings, a
pantry and a sink with running water, which was quite a
modern innovation. The Royal Cambridge Asylum was situated at Kingston-on-Thames and the patrons made frequent
visits not only to preside over the management committees
but also as ladies bountiful to distribute 'comforts' such as tea
and sugar. They called on those who were sick and gave
special presents on such occasions as the anniversary of the
death of the Duke of Cambridge or to commemorate the
fortunate escape of the Duchess of Cambridge from a carriage
accident. The family's interest in the asylum continued unabated even after the death of the old duchess and of Princess
Mary herself. In addition to this special charitable interest,
Princess Mary was actively involved early in her married life
in promoting the establishment of a school in Bermondsey
and a home at Addlestone for females while their parents were
in gaol. She also opened the new orphanage at Watford – some
years previously her father had opened a similar institution at
Clapton – and she happily accepted the £10,000 subscription
raised on its behalf. At one time or another in her life she was

to be patroness of such institutions as the London Homeopathic Hospital, the Governess's Benevolent Institution, the National Orthopedic Hospital, the National Society for Prevention to Cruelty to Children, the National Hospital for the Paralyzed and Epileptic, the German Hospital, the Orphan Working School, the Royal Female Asylum, the Royal School for the Daughters of Officers of the Army and the Theatrical Mission. There were numerous other bodies as well with which she was involved. In every case, Princess Mary was an active participant, never willing merely to give only nominal support through the use of her name and her position. Indeed, it is with her role in charitable activities that she embodies the new function of royalty in an increasingly bourgeois society.

Life was not all confined to duty and Princess Mary and her husband continued to make expeditions to the continent. Rumpenheim was a regular stopping place as was Stuttgart. The Tecks took their children on some of these holidays thereby extending their horizons and also making them aware of their royal connections. One summer they went to Oberammergau to see *The Passion Play*. It lasted seven hours and Princess Mary felt the production to be 'soul-stirring' and presented 'by simple peasants with a truth, a solemnity, a simplicity, and a grandeur'. She felt it made one 'realise so vividly the death and passion of our Saviour' and it enabled one to 'understand the Bible better'.

No sojourn abroad was complete without a holiday in Strelitz and the company of her aunt, sister, brother-in-law and nephew. To some, Strelitz may have been dull but the Tecks and especially the Duke, were much drawn to a society that was based on an appreciation and correctness of the social order. Rank and privilege were unquestioned and respect was always to one's betters. Princess Mary was particularly fond of celebrating her birthday in Strelitz for the local people as well as those who were part of the court circle were very fond of her and were agreeably deferential while extending their greetings. Christmas and New Year festivities in this remote part of Germany were very much ritualized and part of the pleasure in being at Strelitz was in knowing that things were traditional and unchanging.

Just prior to the Tecks' arrival in Strelitz in the autumn of 1873, the Duchess of Cambridge was stricken with a stroke while staying with her elder daughter, Princess Augusta, but while severely paralyzed for a time she does not seem to have lost her speech. However, the patient was more or less confined to her rooms over the holidays and could not be present when the present tables were unveiled; she recovered somewhat and after a couple of months was up and about, but thereafter she was very much of an invalid. Indeed, like many of her contemporaries she tended to revel in 'poor health', and to make demands on her family. When she returned home the responsibility for entertaining and amusing her fell on Princess Mary and her children who were required to visit her frequently.

For one last time the Duchess had to face the prospect of a lengthy journey and the 'awful' thought of the Channel. Of the journey, Lady Geraldine observed, '*Forty* unbroken hours... she suffered terribly'. However, the Duchess was not as fragile as those around her believed and she quickly recovered her general equanimity. She took up residence at Cambridge Cottage where she tried to revive the pattern of life before her illness but, being less mobile and active, she found existence in the country too limiting especially because she liked society. By late 1874 she decided to remove herself permanently to her apartments at St James's Palace where she would be more accessible to her family and friends. Princess Mary called nearly every day whenever she was in London, and she never seems to have found these duties irksome. The Duke of Cambridge also saw his mother almost daily, walking over from The Horse Guards on his way to Gloucester House. The Teck boys were less involved than their sister as they were off at school. However, during the holidays Princess Mary was assiduous in requiring their company on her visits to 'dear grandmamma'. The younger generation were often bored with the dreary teas, the required recitation of 'Sunday Scripture lessons' and joining in the singing of lugubrious hymns with doleful titles such as 'Thy Will be Done'. The Duchess's grandchildren were very much in awe of the old lady and conversation did not flow easily. Moreover, the presence of Lady Geraldine Somerset did not encourage cosy amiability.

With the Duchess of Cambridge comfortably ensconced in St James's Palace, Princess Mary encouraged family and friends to come to see her. One relative who accepted her niece's invitation was Aunt Marie, the Dowager Grand Duchess of Mecklenburg-Strelitz, who, although seventy-nine, braved the Channel. The Duchess of Cambridge and her daughter found Aunt Marie's company delightful but 'the dear invalid' was not always pleased when she was left alone when 'dear Tante Marie' wanted to see the sights and meet other people; to Princess Mary her aunt was 'most enterprising' and 'a perfect marvel for her age'. While successful enough Aunt Marie's visit was only a temporary diversion for her sister and after her departure Princess Mary once more assumed the role of being the principal resource for her mother's entertainment.

Although of the Queen's generation, Princess Mary was really more part of the world of her children. She and Prince Francis frequently were guests at functions in Marlborough House. However, Princess Mary was not always at her ease with the Prince of Wales for at one moment he was 'matey' and at another 'excessively royal'; while he could often be charmingly informal on occasion, at any indication that his rank and position were somehow not properly appreciated he could become quite difficult. Moreover, his 'chaffing manner', part teasing and part serious, baffled his cousin Princess Mary. She could not cope with this sort of behaviour as it was really outside her experience. On the other hand, it has been said that the Prince of Wales was slightly afraid of her, partly because of her size, partly because of her being of another generation and partly because of her manner which he could

H.R.H. Albert Edward, Prince of Wales, later King Edward VII, the cousin of Princess Mary, always slightly intimidated her. He had met the Prince of Teck in Austria and had brought him to England.
(From Review of Reviews — private collection)

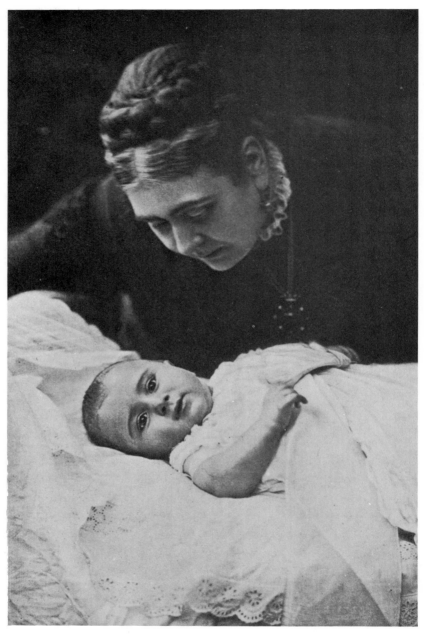

*H.R.H. Princess Mary and her son H.S.H. Prince Alexander, later Earl of Athlone.
(Photograph by W.D. Downey — courtesy John Murray)*

not comprehend: she could mix equally freely with all classes so successfully. With the Princess of Wales the situation was less difficult. For one thing, her family were habitués of Rumpenheim, her mother was a niece of the Duchess of Cambridge, and the princess was sincerely fond of her English relations. The more so since the Cambridges were all anti-Prussian and had supported the Danes during the war in 1864. In addition, Princess Alexandra was essentially kind and generous; she could understand, too, the ambivalent position of the Duke of Teck in society and was ever ready to show the world that he was very much part of the royal family. Princess Mary returned Princess Alexandra's regard, 'She is a very great darling and I *just adore her.*' There were many visits to Sandringham and dinners and receptions at Marlborough House. Since the Prince and Princess of Wales were well-off everything was done with great style and *panache*. There was a chicness about everything they did which the Tecks could never attain but they enjoyed and appreciated them nevertheless. Both Princess Mary and her husband liked the grand manner and the Prince of Wales was a past master. The children of the two families became quite intimate but Princess Mary's sons and daughter had a more normal less cloying home life, and were exposed to more varied society. The offspring of the Prince of Wales were not very well educated. While the three Teck boys were sent off to school, the elder two to Wellington and the youngest to Eton, Prince Eddy and Prince George and their sisters, on the other hand, were all a bit childish because of their mother's sentimental manner.

The Princesses Louise, Victoria and Maud never seemed to learn the truth of their Aunt Marie Edinburgh's dictum, 'Nothing is more hopeless than a Princess who never opens her mouth.' On the other hand, Princess Mary expected her children to move easily in society and to cope successfully in a variety of social situations as she could do herself. Nevertheless, she thought children were children as can be seen in her comment, 'A child has enough to do... to learn obedience, and attend to... lessons, and to *grow* without many parties

Princess Mary and her husband the Duke of Teck and their daughter Princess May in the gardens at Kensington Palace. (From the collection of H.M. The Queen)

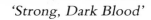
freshness of childhood away....
children in the present day.'
about the Prince of Wales, on
m and held him in great affec-
when he had typhoid fever in
She noted after receiving the
ied over the almost hopeless
ke of the end as not far distant
at once rally' and later in a letter
te sincere when she said, 'The merciful
d Prince... made our Christmas a *more*
one.'

se and its denizens attracted the Tecks
ays it symbolized all that they would
s no question of rank, no problem of
position and future. Neither Princess
is, however, ever showed any outward
at times it cannot have been easy for
th the sort of hospitality they received
ations. For example, the Tecks were
scene at the splendid fancy dress ball
1874 with Princess Mary as part of the
Prince Francis in the *Vandyke*. In this
hostess shared pride of place with the
re but not one that could be returned.
pitality was rather more intimate and
ie Wales' children were always wel-
ad Kensington Palace and they were
the kindness and hospitality they
from that at Marlborough House. It
d, and although the Tecks' position
oyals never failed to call. This cour-
he Empress Elizabeth of Austria
shy') the Queen of the Belgians ('we
ffee and tea!') Aunt Marie of Meck-
Londres') the Queen of Greece ('dear
ed Empress Eugénie ('a great friend') were all

received with enthusiasm. However, the Duke of Teck was bored with his existence; he was never allowed to do anything constructive. Disraeli proposed to the Queen that the Tecks might be sent to Ireland as viceroy and vicereine but this was not approved. In fact the way of life was essentially shallow and superficial. Moreover, it was expensive and the claims of creditors could not be resisted forever. Prince Francis hated the idea of economizing. To him it was somehow degrading having to be concerned with money. His daughter was to say later, 'Poor man, if only he was less proud and foolish about that sort of thing, what can it matter how many servants one has as long as one can live comfortably?' To the Duke of Teck it mattered a great deal. He noted, 'My own liabilities are not greater than any other gentleman about town.' This was no solution to anything. The princess, on the other hand, could delude herself that her existence was meaningful, she had her mother and her charities. She recognized her husband's dilemma but would or could do nothing to alleviate it and continued outwardly serene and unconcerned. Despite the occasional gloomy outbursts of the Duke of Teck, life seemed destined to be unchanged. Of course there was the scare when their daughter caught typhoid – obviously the drains in royal residences were inadequate – but fortunately she recovered. There was vast enthusiasm when Doppus of Mecklenburg 'dear Gussy's' only child became engaged in the winter of 1877. 'We were completely taken by surprise,' wrote his aunt. The visits to the continent were annual affairs as were the sojourns in the country houses of their aristocratic friends. The Duke and Duchess of Teck seemed generally oblivous of the realities of life in the larger sense. The shallowness of their existence was not observed because they were 'royal' and because somehow they had always managed to cope with the worst of their financial crises. They lived as they believed they were required to live to maintain their position and because to change it would have required an effort that might have been disagreeable.

However, the apparent casualness with respect to economic matters could not continue. Queen Victoria, aware of the general indifference of Princess Mary about debt, had always declined to increase her income. The princess was the responsibility of her own family; however, there were complications because the Duke of Cambridge had his three sons to support, and was apparently very generous to his good friend Louisa Beauclark, of whom Princess Mary observed darkly that she 'absorbed all he could give'. This was not quite true but it did provide an excuse for the Duke's reluctance to help his sister because he knew there would be no end.

The Teck income was not really so inadequate if it were properly managed. Princess Mary now had an allowance from the country of £5,000; there was another £2,000 from the widowed Duchess of Cambridge. The sum of £7,000 a year meant that the Tecks, while not rich, were comfortable, had they been more practical. Over the years the Duchess of Cambridge had given extra sums. Since 1866 it was reckoned that she had provided her younger daughter with at least £2,000 a year in addition to the £2,000 she added to Princess Mary's parliamentary grant. Friends had been generous as well but the Tecks failed to comprehend that they were getting more and more deeply in debt. While family and friends might never have pressed for repayment – they probably recognized that they would never be able to collect what was owed to them – other people were less benign. Monies owed to shopkeepers had to be paid and when the latter began to complain, it was evident that desperate methods were required. The Tecks remained oblivious apparently. They complained that the family was stingy and lacked understanding with all suggestions about the need to economize being rejected. Princess Mary had no intention of giving up her way of life. She resolutely declined to consider having only one establishment – everyone had a pied-à-terre in town and 'a place'; any other arrangement was quite impossible. Did her brother not have Gloucester House and Cambridge Cottage? Family pressure continued and this had the momentary effect of depressing the Tecks. Princess Mary wrote to a friend on one occasion, 'I am very low, having very much to try me.' By this she meant her mother, brother and sister were badgering her to be less extravagant but she continued, 'I am looking for the silver lining to the dark cloud... I keep as brave a heart as I can.'

One obvious solution was for the Tecks to retire to the continent where life was less expensive. This was frequently done by families wishing to economize. Brussels at one time was very popular, Germany was another alternative. Indeed, Queen Victoria's own parents had lived abroad for a time to save money. The Queen was obviously the only person who could force the issue but even she was beguiled by her cousin who presented quite another story to that which she had heard from the Cambridges. According to Princess Mary the latter were really very unfeeling, especially her brother and sister, and were quite cruel in their attacks on the Teck household. For a brief time the Queen wavered but finally even she decided to be firm; Kensington Palace was to be given up permanently and White Lodge retained but the Tecks would have to accept a stay on the continent in order to retrench and recoup their finances. After a valiant rearguard action Princess Mary and her husband finally accepted the situation. However, Princess Mary was much depressed. In a letter to her friend Lady Aylesford, she said, 'I do my best to keep up my spirits and make myself pleasant; for, alas! a great trial is before me... we are going... to Kensington Palace to wind up there, and break up the beautiful happy home, that has sheltered us for the last *sixteen* years and in which all our children were born.' She concluded by saying, 'You can guess the wrench it will be to us...'.

On 15th September 1883 the Tecks accompanied by their children departed from London. To ensure there were no mishaps and no sudden changes of plan the Duke of Cambridge and his sister, the Grand Duchess Augusta, were present. Apparently everyone was quite serene and cheerful except for the Grand Duchess who was in tears despite having been one of the strongest advocates for the withdrawal of the

Tecks from England. The ubiquitous Lady Geraldine Somerset observed, 'It all went off far better and quieter than I had feared... No tears no scene'. It would almost seem as if Lady Geraldine would have preferred 'a scene' for it would have confirmed her rather negative opinions of Princess Mary and it is apparent that she was annoyed to have been deprived of the satisfaction of seeing her discomfited.

Her Majesty Queen Victoria in early middle life. She was a great ally of Princess Mary although at times the latter exasperated the Queen with her unpunctuality and failure to answer letters.
(From the collection of H.M. The Queen — photograph by B.E. Dupper)

CHAPTER FOUR

Domestic Bliss

When they travelled, royalty periodically went incognito. It was really a sort of fiction because everyone knew who they were. On occasion, Queen Victoria used the title the Countess of Balmoral and Edward VII was called Baron Renfrew. The Tecks and their family used the name of Hohenstein, the name he had held until he assumed the Teck title. Nobody, of course, was naive enough to believe that the Hohensteins were anything but royals in mufti; besides, Princess Mary was so well known and so readily recognized that she could not be anyone but herself.

The English relatives of the Tecks hoped that they would settle in Graz near the Duke's sister or in Frankfurt with their Württemberg cousins. Besides a sojourn in Württemberg might induce the Tecks to consider having one or all of their sons take up a military career there thus providing these impoverished princes with an occupation. The idea never appealed to Princess Mary and was firmly rejected. She very wisely felt they were better off in England where they would never be subjected to the slights and snubs that were meted out to 'the imperfect royals' by their German connections. Prince Francis concurred with this view as he was so obsessed by the question of rank and privilege. At the court of Queen Victoria they were more secure and more sure of a happy future.

It is evident that the princess and her family had no intention of living quietly and in obscurity even if this were the ostensible reason for their sojourn on the continent. Instead they acted as if they were merely going on their usual holiday and they went to the Villa Seefeld which belonged to Princess Catherine of Württemberg. She had always doted on Francis Teck and was delighted to have him and his family as her guests. Life at Villa Seefeld on Lake Constance was not too dissimilar to that at Rumpenheim with cheerful excursions, picnics and family gatherings. However, the Villa was really only a temporary halt because the Tecks had decided to go on to Florence, in spite of Queen Victoria's disapproval on the account of expense: 'Some quieter and more retired spot would have been better.'

Villa Seefeld was vacated in mid-October and five days later they reached Florence. They made several stops and everywhere were greeted with full honours as Her Royal Highness and His Serene Highness – so much for the incognito. Indeed, an invitation to dine with King Humbert at his country house at Monza simply underscored the fact that nobody was prepared to receive the Count and Countess Hohenstein as ordinary mortals. Indeed, they even travelled to Monza in a special train with the king's own railway carriage. Princess Mary was delighted by King Humbert's reception of her and the Duke. It was obviously not an exile but a progress.

When the Tecks reached Florence they went to Paoli's Hotel, an establishment much favoured by the English – it had 'certain English comforts' – because the proprietor had been in the employ of Sir James Hudson, who was the British Minister to the Tuscan court prior to the setting up of the Kingdom of Italy. The Tecks began moderately enough with only a suite of rooms but they quickly expanded to take in the entire floor to be sure that no strange person was near by. This increase of accommodation added to the cost but such trifles were not significant to Princess Mary. Prince Francis, however, was to be less pleased when the bills were submitted; apparently the Tecks simply assumed that Paoli would oblige them by letting them use the extra space without charge.

Life at the hotel began to take on many of the aspects of Kensington Palace or White Lodge. There were courtesy calls made by Italian officials, English residents, distinguished foreign denizens of the city and German cousins. The Tecks were enthusiastic visitors to museums and places of local interest, for example, they went to the Villa Petraria where they saw the rooms of Princess Mary's former suitor, King Victor Emmanuel, just as he had left them. A poignant reminder of the past and a rather macabre custom among royal families – a remembrance of 'the dear departed'. They patronized the opera, where the royal box was placed at their disposal, and the philharmonic society. Prince Francis availed himself of the amenities of the Florence Club – he later became the Honorary President – which boasted a membership made up chiefly of English and American visitors. Princess Mary busied herself with good causes, distributing prizes for the local humane society, giving certificates of proficiency on behalf of the St John Ambulance Association, attending benefit concerts for poor Spanish students and visiting hospital workhouses. One for orphans and old people was described by Princess Mary as 'wonderfully clean for Italy, well aired and well kept'. All of these activities were very much the same as in London. As in the past when Princess Mary had accompanied her mother on continental tours, her daughter's routine of lessons continued under the direction of Fräulein Gutmann, a rather tiresome and somewhat incompetent preceptress.

Nobody for one minute was able to pretend the Tecks were a mere Count and Countess Hohenstein. Princess Mary 'was everywhere received as a Royal Princess,' one observer noted, 'the claims of etiquette only being replaced by Her Royal Highness's gracious simplicity and cordiality of manner, which her tranquil dignity never permitted·to be misunderstood.'

Florence was hardly a social Siberia; there were charming Russians – the fabulous Princess Worontsow with her superb pearls, the attractive Prince Wolkonsky whom they had met on the journey from Graz, the Countess de Talleyrand married to a French husband and a Princess Gortschakow who was a relation of the Imperial chancellor. The French were well represented with the Dukes de Dino and de Chartres and Count de Talleyrand. There were shoals of upper class

English, among them the Earl and Countess of Crawford, Lady Caroline Ricketts and her daughters, Lady Orford who had a salon, the Shaw-Stewarts, and even old Sir James Hudson, the former minister. The old Tuscan noble families such as the Marchese Medici, the Marchese Montagliari, the Count and Countess Corti and the Marchese Ginori and his brother-in-law the Marchese Torrigiani, all of them welcomed their distinguished visitors with enthusiasm. The Tecks did not just surround themselves with grandees but received as they had in London. Interesting people joined their circle, the Colnaghi family from London, Miss Susan Horner, the authoress of a guidebook about Florence and who acted as a guide for Princess Mary and her daughter on their tours, Mrs Manson (a friend from England), Mrs Janet Ross the great rival to the 'dreadful Ouida' and an agreeable young American painter Henry Thaddeus Jones – 'Mr Thaddy', who became a great favourite with the whole household. The Princess's journal is full of reports of outings: a concert in the Palazzo Rinuccini, tea with the Colnaghis, an evening at Villa la Colombia – 'Dinner exquis!' – dances at the Palazzo Riccardi and the like. Perhaps it can all be summed up in her comment about her birthday,

'Up before eight but hindered in my dressing by letters, telegrams and flowers! At twelve o'clock I received my presents in the drawing room; chocolate *lunch* directly afterwards, at one went... to the Duomo... The Cathedral was opened for me... From 2:30 I had quite a levée and my lovely flowers – baskets, cushions and bouquets of all dimensions – very much admired... We had a very cheery little dinner, and in the evening the William Rumbolds and Colnaghi ladies came, and we had some music... Wolkonsky played a valse, and we *all* danced away till about twelve or so, when the party broke up. Very nice day!'

Lady Geraldine Somerset would have vastly disapproved for this was hardly what she and her royal mistress, the Duchess of Cambridge, would have described as living in a 'smaller way'.

Christmas was celebrated as usual with all the family together, the elder sons having come from school in England. The new year opened with no diminution of Princess Mary's social life with teas, receptions, dinners and expeditions. However, this delightful existence was halted when suddenly Prince Francis was taken ill. On the morning of 5th March, he awakened to find himself partially paralysed; his wife's reaction was to reject the obvious, namely that he had had a stroke, and to assume that he was suffering from an attack of nerves or from sunstroke. Fortunately he quickly made a partial recovery. Within less than a fortnight he was up and about and able to walk a short distance. With her ability to perceive only that which suited her, Princess Mary was certain that her husband would soon be fully fit and that the sombre accounts that her relations were spreading were complete fabrications. To give the lie to the reports that Prince Francis was severely ill, Princess Mary quickly resumed her usual activities with her journal being filled with accounts of picnics, local fêtes and receptions that she attended. Her buoyant optimism was infectious and Prince Francis soon began to take a renewed interest in life. To hasten his recovery he left the hotel and retired to the country accepting the hospitality of the owner of the Villa Stibbert.

Princess Mary took the opportunity of completing a project that she and her husband had long considered, namely, a removal from Florence and the acquisition of a villa nearby. Their financial situation was still as chaotic as ever and they really had no ready money to rent a suitable house. All of the royal affability that Princess Mary had displayed now had its own rewards. Miss Bianca Light whose family had owned a villa for over four decades offered to lend it to the Tecks for as long as they cared to occupy it. This was generosity indeed; Miss Light herself used only a few rooms and then only intermittently; therefore, the Tecks virtually had the place for themselves. Moreover, Miss Light paid the basic expenses as the essential staff were in her employment; only the cook's wages and those of their personal attendants were charged to the Tecks. Obviously, the Villa I Cedri had everything to commend it; above all there was no rent to pay – Princess Mary had spent nearly £2,000 in the previous three months – and it was an exceptionally good place to hasten the full recovery of Prince Francis. The house and its surrounding gardens were to be as Princess Mary wrote in her diary 'a charming spring abode for us' and one which they were to occupy for a year.

The Villa I Cedri was situated in the environs of Florence itself, close enough for friends to come and enjoy its amenities and yet rural enough to be thoroughly rustic. When Prince Francis arrived – his wife and daughter and younger son had left Paoli's Hotel at the beginning of April – he was much pleased with it. All that is required was his touch with the interior furnishing to make it quite perfect. This new rustic retreat very quickly became 'home' and was to be regarded as the White Lodge in a Tuscan setting.

All of Florentine society as well as the numerous visitors and royal relations who passed through the city came to call. Princess Mary's journal is replete with the names of friends and acquaintances who were her guests. Musical evenings were frequent, teas in the garden a daily occurrence while the dinner parties 'were remarkable for their whole-hearted gaiety'. Friends noted that Princess Mary 'was a delightful hostess... [and] at I Cedri entertained in the most charming and hospitable manner'. Thaddeus Jones the American artist observed that Princess Mary was 'so genial and gracious' and added a universal comment: 'All were made welcome'. The sojourn at I Cedri brought out the very best in the Tecks – their affability, geniality, hospitality and real kindness. Because of their numerous social and domestic obligations Princess Mary indulged herself in putting aside chores which bored her. Her correspondence, never kept up well, tended to lapse and this irritated her mother and also Queen Victoria. When finally forced out of her lassitude she resorted to the telegraph as a means of communicating with her family. It is said she once sent off a telegram of twenty-six pages in length. Even her kind sister was irritated and observed, 'As for your never writing it really is beyond comprehension! This is my 4th letter...'

If inclined to please herself in many matters she was vitally concerned about her husband. He made a gradual improvement but it was clear that he remained a difficult invalid. Some sort of holiday away from the heat of Florence was required, various projects were considered. Bad Gastein and Rumpenheim were proposed, but they were rejected. After some further correspondence with the Duchess of Cambridge, the Tecks agreed to go to Seelisbergen on Lake Lucerne. The family had a suite at the Hotel Sonenberg where Prince Francis was to have *Heil-gymnastick*.

As the days went by, Princess Mary observed that Prince Francis was bored and quickly acted to rectify the situation. She wrote to a friend named Peter Wells whom they knew in Florence pointing out that her husband was lonely and asked if he could come to stay. She asked, 'Could you take a *frisk* up here for a fortnight or so?' adding that if he came to Switzerland, Prince Francis would have some society. The invitation was accepted and later Thaddeus Jones came as well. After his illness Prince Francis was more easily irritated and more inclined to irascibility. His temper became shorter and he was less easy. At no time did Princess Mary ever complain and she and the children did everything to soothe his nerves and to make life pleasant for him despite his touchiness on almost every subject.

With good company Prince Francis was more inclined to enjoy the stay in Switzerland and this meant that life for his wife was more agreeable also. Princess Mary was able to write in early August, 'Left dear Sonnenberg *très à regret*' – earlier the hotel had been described as being not very commodious, 'with a rather shaky balcony' and somewhat overcrowded with noisy German tourists. After leaving Lake Lucerne they made their way to Bad Horn on the Bodensee where once again they stayed at a hotel but spent much of their time at Villa Seefeld. Life at Bad Horn was simple and easy; it was a bit dull for Princess Mary but not for her children and husband. She preferred a more active existence with plenty of people to entertain her. However, evenings at the Villa Seefeld were not totally unamusing being like those spent at I Cedri with card games, music, charades and conversation. A more exciting evening occurred when Prince Francis accidentally set a coach house on fire – described by Princess Mary as 'Such fun!' The house party also indulged themselves in table turning which amused them all hugely as it jumped about the room. Of course, meals were also important consisting of many courses and taking interminable time to consume.

Even while partaking of rural pleasures, the Tecks never failed to remember their position and rank. Prince Francis liked to be able to allude to the Württemberg sovereigns as 'cousins' and therefore it was their duty to pay their respects to the elderly King Charles of Württemberg and his wife, Queen Olga. The latter was a daughter of Tsar Nicholas I of Russia and was very proud of her family. In her youth she was reckoned to be dazzlingly beautiful but as she grew older she became extremely thin and rather frightening. She had brains and energy which her husband lacked. He was a weak man, not as significant in German politics as his father had been, and was thought by his contemporaries to be mentally unbalanced. Württemberg like Strelitz was very formal, court etiquette was rigid in the extreme and for Princess Mary a bore and a trial. The official visit with the three boys and Princess May went off all right but everyone was happy when it was over. King Charles and Queen Olga had been scrupulously polite but the whole ambience served once more to convince Princess Mary how lucky she had been not to marry into 'one of the small German courts' and how wise was the decision to make the Teck Princes to be, as Princess Mary said

H.M. Queen Olga of Württemberg, wife of King Charles. She disliked the Teck family and was probably influential in preventing Prince Francis from receiving the title of Duke of Württemberg or royal rank. Queen Olga was a daughter of Tsar Nicholas I of Russia and a very proud and imperious woman.
(From a miniature on ivory in the collection of H.M. Queen Beatrix of the Netherlands)

to an old friend, 'thorough English boys' rather than as potential officers in the Württemberg army where formal etiquette ruled all behaviour.

Much more engaging was the holiday at Gmunden with the exiled King George of Hanover and his family. The head of the House of Guelph was married to a sister of Princess Alexandra of Wales and so the entire establishment was strongly anti-Prussian. Gmunden was Rumpenheim all over again, hordes of cousins, jolly rural picnics, teas in the garden and musical evenings. The 'royal mob' was very much in evidence and their obvious enjoyment in the relaxed atmosphere and in each other's company was delightful to observe.

Before returning to Florence, the Tecks revisited Graz to see Prince Francis' two sisters because the latter had not seen their brother and sister-in-law for over a decade. Princess Claudine had become more eccentric with more animals to command her attention. Princess Amelia had obviously taken her brother's advice about Schloss Reinthal and in the opinion of both Princess Mary and her husband, it was 'much improved, as regards furnishing and comfort'.

The lengthy sojourn away from Florence ended in late November when the family took up residence once more at Villa I Cedri. The winter of 1884 was spent much as in the past with dinners, soirées and the like. From all appearances it would seem as if Princess Mary had determined to remain in Italy for an extended period but in fact she was anxious to get home to White Lodge. However, when matters were so arranged that she could go back to England, she did not accept with alacrity indicating instead her desire of remaining at least until May. This apparent change of heart rather surprised her mother who had been led to believe that nothing was more important to her daughter than an immediate return to London.

Princess Mary was unapologetic about her change of plan and amused herself as usual. The journal for April records such things as a visit to the Church of San Lorenzo for the services for Maundy Thursday 'saw the Archbishop's entry...

and seeing him washing the feet of thirty old men (the ceremony, as usual, did not impress me')…. On another day she 'found Khedive Ismail with his son…. Très amiable!' and on another 'drove to town… to order a cottage piano for the hall, and called at Darcy's for dishes and bonbons… at 9:30 we went to supper, nineteen in the drawing room and twelve in the dining room… were very merry and quite sorry to break up, which we did about 12:30.' The happy days at Villa I Cedri were finally at an end. Princess Mary bade farewell to the large and congenial circle in Florence. She and the family packed up to go home. The plan was for them to arrive in England at the end of May in time to celebrate their daughter's eighteenth birthday. Unfortunately just prior to their departure, Princess Mary had a fall and owing to her size and weight, she injured herself quite seriously. Everthing had to be delayed for several days and consequently they only reached London the actual birthday itself so anything more than a family dinner was quite impossible.

Despite the fact that her mother, brother and sister as well as the Queen all felt some doubts as to whether she and her husband had learned frugality in Italy, Princess Mary was given a warm and enthusiastic welcome. They regretted leaving Florence to be sure but White Lodge was 'home' and at this season of the year it was looking particularly agreeable. Nevertheless they did not move immediately into White Lodge but stayed for a brief time at Alford House, lent to them by their old friend, Lady Marian Alford, and later Chester Square. The Chester Square house was not particularly commodious and furnished in a rather grim way but as usual Prince Francis rearranged everything to his own liking and friends came to call. In a letter to Peter Wells in Florence, the Duke said 'We hope to stay a little time in town, and indeed it does one good to see everyone smile their greeting from carriages and foot paths, and waving their hands'. What was obviously particularly gratifying was that their house was the object of 'a regular pilgrimage to Princess Mary's door, and hundreds of people have been to write their names down here'. It was very evident that Princess Mary was far from being forgotten and upon her return could not complain of neglect.

They had hoped for an amusing London season, the highlight of which would be their daughter's presentation at court. However, they were to be prevented from enjoying themselves by the unexpected death of the Duke of Teck's father. Princess Mary's comments on the event are revealing. 'Alas! our pleasant dinner on Wednesday, and the dance on Friday for poor May, are over.... I dread the effect of the journey to Vienna for Francis, in this intense heat, and only hope the Doctor will forbid his going.' Duke Alexander of Württemberg's demise would mean that six months of mourning were required; moreover, it meant that Prince Francis would have to attend his funeral and, as his daughter remarked, considering 'that his brain feels as though loose and moving in his head,' it would be impossible for him to go alone. After consulting his medical advisors, Princess Mary's views were confirmed. He was not well enough to travel and it was agreed that he might be represented by his two older sons. The latter had little sentiment for their grandfather, nor indeed does Prince Francis seem to have mourned him much. The old Duke had no money, he lived in a tiny house, his possessions were simple, only sentimental souvenirs of the past, but his death did allow Princes Adolphus and Francis the excuse for a sojourn in Vienna which it seems they vastly enjoyed.

Duke Alexander's death was more of an inconvenience than anything because mourning demanded that all social life had to be curtailed which irritated Princess Mary. For example, she could not attend the wedding of Princess Beatrice and this was particularly galling as 'the royal mob' was very much in evidence. Besides, Princess Beatrice like herself, was marrying one who was 'imperfectly royal' and for Princess Mary, participation at the nuptials would have given her considerable satisfaction. For the Tecks this was a really tangible sign that Queen Victoria did not regard *ebenbürtig* status as being important. Princess Mary was always annoyed that her husband was never regarded by his German relations as a true *Hocheit*; the Battenberg marriage was convincing proof that in England at least the Tecks were truly part of the real royal circle.

While in mourning the Princess Mary and her husband retired to White Lodge, now their only home, but they soon resumed the pattern of existence that they had had before going to Florence. Prince Francis amused himself with restoring the garden and suitably placing the family furniture that was formerly in London. Such occupations, considering the general uncertainty of his health, were deemed to be quite exciting enough. Indeed, the mourning period for Duke Alexander perhaps imposed a needed respite from the efforts of the return to London, and the activities involved with life in England. The only break in the retirement came with the confirmation of Princess May and her eldest brother in August. This event, while a solemn one, was also very pleasurable for the young people, both of whom received handsome presents from the family. There was a luncheon party given by the Duchess of Cambridge for her grandchildren after the service which had taken place in the Chapel Royal. With Princess May's confirmation completed, Princess Mary could now look forward to her daughter's presentation at court. This occurred in the spring of 1886 at a drawing room where Queen Victoria treated Princess May as a 'regular royal princess' totally disregarding the fact that to her continental relations, she was 'imperfectly royal'. Naturally, this sign of approbation delighted both Princess Mary and Prince Francis with their concern for status. Earlier in the same year, Princess Mary and Princess May attended the state opening of parliament and were seated on the Woolsack; this also implied, of course, that Queen Victoria accepted the Princess Mary's daughter as a full member of the Blood Royal. From these incidents and the other public state occasions, it was clear that Princess Mary's family were highly placed in any English order of precedence.

H.S.H. Princess Mary (Princess May) the only daughter of Princess Mary and the Duke of Teck at the time of her marriage. (From Review of Reviews — private collection)

Summer was spent at White Lodge but in the autumn Princess Mary and her husband once more made a round of country house visits. This was an annual event and helped to make Princess Mary so popular with society. They stayed at Rufford, Thoresby, Hardwicke and at Cragside. The last of these large establishments was owned by Sir William Armstrong, the armaments maker, and it was all very modern. It appears that at Cragside Princess Mary finally was introduced to modern lighting. In a letter to Lady Tankerville, she wrote, 'Sir William initiated me into the mysteries of turning the electric light on and off, which sheds a charming light from one centre drop, or jet, over the whole room – a good sized one'.

After their three week holiday, they returned to White Lodge 'greatly refreshed by the change,' Princess Mary said. While she had really learned very little about economy in Florence, she was slightly, but only slightly, less improvident than previously. Nevertheless she and her husband continued to entertain on what would now seem a lavish scale and to maintain a sizeable staff. Princess Mary's domestic arrangements were always satisfactory, but she was as disorganized as ever in her private affairs. The arrival of Hélène Bricka improved the situation somewhat, the correspondence was more regularly attended to and things were completed on time. Punctuality was not something Princess Mary ever understood and here she was, like her cousin the Princess of Wales. Indeed, it is because of the latter's inability to be on time for anything that the so-called 'Sandringham time', that is the clocks all being advanced one half-hour, was devised.

The Golden Jubilee Year of Queen Victoria was celebrated in great style by everyone both in Britain and the Empire. The Tecks were part of the royal procession. They and two German princes were in one carriage, their children in another, and they all received many hearty cheers. Princess Mary in particular was very well known – 'fat Mary' as she was referred to affectionately – and she liked the public's approbation. Indeed, the Empress Frederick believed she courted it.

Her own explanation was more ingenious: 'as one of the old royal family the kind public always gave me a warm welcome and I am very proud of it'. Part of her popularity was the result of her involvement with numerous charities and the Jubilee provided the excuse for more such activities. The family connection with the Royal Cambridge Asylum was rigorously maintained. The London Needlework Guild which made clothing for the poor practically had its headquarters at White Lodge. Princess Mary was not merely a patroness but a real participant. She enjoyed prize-giving and organizing bazaars. In late November 1887, for example, she was actively involved in raising money for a vicarage at Petersham and cheerfully recorded in a lengthy letter to Peter Wells, an old friend of Florence days, that the event was 'a great success in every way and realized £250'. She was just as happy performing a public duty on a relatively humble level as being the lady bountiful and royal personage on the larger scene.

Since her daughter was now 'out' she could accompany Princess Mary on those numerous progresses the latter enjoyed so much. The boys were now more or less settled. Dolly was gazetted to the 17th Hussars and after a sojourn in Württemberg he was to join his regiment in London. Princess Mary was always concerned that her children kept up their languages. Indeed, Queen Victoria was much perturbed that the younger denizens of Marlborough House was not properly fluent in German. The Queen deplored the attitude taken by her son and daughter-in-law on this matter and was much pleased that Princess Mary kept up the traditions properly. Prince Frank was at Sandhurst and Prince Alge was at Eton.

After the official celebrations of the Golden Jubilee, there was a house party at Luton Hoo, the residence of de Falbe, the Danish Minister, and Princess Mary and her daughter joined the other guests, Lady Howe, Colonel Byng and his two girls, some relations of their host and hostess, a Danish count and a Mrs Williams and her stepson. The latter was back in England from a ranch in Texas. Princess Mary was informed that it did not pay but that it was an interesting place and life there exciting. The entertainment was simple – dinner parties for twenty, whist and other card games, dancing to an organ, tennis in the afternoon, strolls in the garden and fishing in the lake. Expeditions were made to neighbouring country houses and nearby towns. It provided a light relief from the formal activities and events of early June.

Over the years the *Illustrated London News* on its court page reported the numerous visits to country houses made by Princess Mary. It would seem that with the possible exception of the Prince of Wales, no member of the royal family enjoyed the hospitality of the aristocracy as frequently as she and few had as wide and interesting a circle of friends to entertain her.

Life at White Lodge was relatively unchanged from the time before the Tecks went to Florence. However, the Duke still had no settled occupation and as a result of his illness was more fussed over small matters and questions of precedence continued to exercise him. Princess Mary was her charming, agreeable self but in one respect her existence was now more ordered since Mademoiselle Bricka had joined the household in 1886. Mademoiselle Bricka served several functions. She was a sort of governess, and lady companion to Princess May on whom she was to have an excellent influence by broadening her intellectual horizons. She was also to act as secretary to Princess Mary, whose correspondence was considerable, but because of her lack of organization it had often been left unattended. Queen Victoria as well as her mother and sister were frequently critical of Princess Mary's dilatory behaviour. With the advent of Hélène Bricka, things tended to improve generally and particularly with respect to matters relating to the numerous charitable activities patronized by her employer. Private correspondence continued much as before. Indeed, there were frequently piles of letters on tables all over the house awaiting Princess Mary's attention. Moreover, she had the bad habit of dealing with correspondence late at night which inevitably meant that the task was never completed because of her frequent social activities.

In the summer of 1888 the Princess Mary and her family

went to South Wales for their holiday where they were the guests of the Dunravens who very kindly gave the royal visitors a private suite which allowed them to live *en famille* and yet be part of the household. The days were passed much as at Rumpenheim with rural walks and expeditions, visits to local beauty spots and neighbouring country houses, and with music or cards and simple games in the evening. During her stay, Princess Mary also consented to support several local charitable events such as a concert in Swansea.

When Princess Mary returned to London she found that her mother was increasingly frail. The old Duchess of Cambridge managed to get through the winter and it seemed as if she was likely to remain alive for some time but quite suddenly and unexpectedly, she died on 6th April. Princess Mary was not present at her deathbed only being sent for when it was too late. As usual, Princess Augusta was still in Strelitz being on the point of coming to England and the Duke of Cambridge was in Ireland on army business. Of the family, only the Princess of Wales was there to see her great-aunt expire. The end was painless and easy, the Duchess was ninety-three but this did not make the situation any easier. As Queen Victoria observed apropos of her cousin, 'She will feel what she has lost'. Princess Mary was very quickly aware of the gap in her life writing a week after her mother's demise, 'Of the future I dare not think, with its terrible blank, for the one great object and constant care of my life has been taken away'. Later she was to note, 'I really think, as time goes on, and I realize more and more the extent of my bereavement, that having to live on without the precious boon, so long enjoyed, of a mother's enduring love and constant thought, that the sorrow seems to deepen and intensify.' She could console herself with the knowledge that she had been an exceedingly dutiful daughter visiting her aged parent virtually every day when she was in London or at White Lodge and even writing reasonably frequently when she was away.

The funeral was typical of the age. Queen Victoria, who had said on learning of the death of her aunt, 'Now there is

H.M. Ludwig II, King of Bavaria, was a distant relation
of the Duke of Teck. The latter and the Bavarian
monarch were both interested in the arts and in interior
decoration. Both also were ultimately to suffer mental
breakdown.
(Painting by W. Tauber 1864)

H.R.H. The Duchess of Cambridge, the mother of
Princess Mary, in old age. This picture was painted by
Von Angeli who like Winterhalter was very successful in
pleasing his royal patrons. Queen Victoria admired his
work and one of his best pictures is that which he painted
of her.
Engraving in a private collection. Original in the Royal
Collection)

163

nobody left to call me Victoria. And *she* is the *last* above *me*.'
She made a special exception and attended the obsequies
which were held at Kew. The coffin was carried by eight men
from the Grenadier guards while others of the regiment lined
the path to the church. There were many mourners, both
royal as well as official, the ladies were swathed in crepe and
the number of wreaths was quite phenomenal. Queen Victoria
believed her presence was a comfort for the family. 'I am vy
thankful to have been there with my poor Cousins – the two
eldest my contemporaries – and it was a help to them.' The
Queen, assisted by Princess Beatrice, placed a wreath on the
coffin. An era for them all was ended. It was symbolized by
the fact that the Duchess's apartments in St James's Palace
were quickly dismantled, being taken over by Prince Albert
Victor the Duke of Clarence and Avondale the elder son of the
Prince of Wales.

After the court mourning and private family mourning
was ended, Princess Mary accompanied by her daughter went
to Switzerland. She was weary and exhausted with all of the
business of closing up her mother's home; a change was
thought imperative. 'Perfect rest, and bracing air were also
absolutely necessary for me,' she was to write and this was
'found at delightful St Moritz in the Upper Engadine' and
after a sojourn of a month she was completely refreshed and
ready to cope with things anew.

As usual her numerous charitable activities awaited her
attention and there was the round of visits made to various
country houses. Christmas was celebrated as in the past,
although slightly muted because of the death of the Duchess
of Cambridge. Still there were the four present trees: one for
Princess Mary and one for Prince Francis, the third for their
children and the fourth for guests. On Christmas Eve, the
presents were opened and the candles on the trees all lit. A few
days later, the trees were virtually redecorated, presents were
placed at their base and a ceremonial gift-giving for the servants took place.

Early in the new year, the Tecks went off to Luton Hoo –

again they were the guests of the de Falbes – but Princess Mary was taken ill and so further expeditions were curtailed. By early summer Princess Mary, while having recovered from the bout of influenza, was again weary. She evidently had thrown herself back into the affairs of her many charities without realizing the effects of her illness on her general state of health. Another rest in Switzerland was thought the answer and she, her husband, her daughter, and second son, accompanied by Nelson Hood, an equerry and comptroller of the household, went abroad. For once the channel crossing was easy and they then went into a private railway carriage of Alfred Rothschild which was attached to the Brussels train, for a sojourn in the Belgian capital overnight. It was in fact a period of celebration for the sixtieth anniversary of Belgian independence. And they were off to Germany in the morning. Rich people and royal personages were very well treated; private railway carriages were not unusual and at all principal stations there were special waiting rooms for the travellers and officials of the various companies on hand to see to their comfort. They were received in some state even when travelling privately. Nevertheless sometimes things went awry. When Princess Mary and her family and party visited Oberammergau, all they got to eat was a small ham, some cranberry jam and bread. Hardly a festive banquet and all those present were somewhat hungry when they went to bed.

These continental holidays were not short, three weeks at Partenkirchen, six weeks at St Moritz, a fortnight at Schloss Hohenburg and finally nearly two weeks in France. On all of these tours there were meetings with relations like 'Hilda Baden and Vera Württemberg'. The latter seems to have always been moving about accompanied by her plain daughters. There were luncheons, dinners, teas and receptions. Princess Mary used old-fashioned slang to refer to informal dances: 'Duchesse de Luznes *hop*' [author's italics]. There were picnics and other simple pleasures: 'The young people played dumb crambo and charades... I [Princess Mary] went to a bric-a-brac shop and bought a silver hot-water jug for

Princess Mary and her husband, the Duke of Teck, and their four children, circa 1890. The three sons all inherited their father's good looks and were thought to be very handsome young men.
(From a private collection)

Francis.' Almost everything pleased except perhaps Wagner's opera Siegfried 'such a dull wearisome opera – I [Princess Mary] fear I nodded'.

Back home once more the family were pleased to welcome Prince Adolphus on his return from India. 'It is delightful having our dear Indian son at home again, and it was a great joy to see *all* our dear children once more gathered round our dinner-table' and, she added with maternal pride, 'in health and… wonderful good looks!'

In 1888, the Prince and Princess of Wales had celebrated their silver wedding anniversary. A great family dinner was given at Marlborough House and the royal pair were showered with splendid gifts. The Princess of Wales in particular received some superb jewellery. Three years later it was the turn of the Tecks. The event was less a national one for them than that of the Wales's, but the whole family joined in the celebration. Princess Mary, like Princess Alexandra, received jewellery but far more important to the Tecks were the tokens of affection received from less exalted circles, for example, an album of signatures from the local residents of Richmond and its environs testifying the affections in which the Tecks were held, the vast concourse of the grand and the humble at the garden parties at Kew where well-wishers thronged to give the happy pair their greetings. No formal invitations were issued, the Princess and her family just being 'at home' to all and sundry. She added, 'I shall be very pleased to see anyone who may like to come.' Such open generosity was typical. Princess Mary's formal acknowledgement summed up her feelings:

> Deeply touched, deeply grateful to you all, to old and new friends, I offer the fullness of my heart, thanks, which words but can very inadequately express. If I have now and then been able to render some service… I remember what pleasure it has given me, and ever will give me.

H.R.H. Princess Augusta, Grand Duchess of Mecklenburg-Strelitz the sister of Princess Mary. Princess Augusta was always much more grand than her younger sister.
(Photograph by Ellis & Woley from a private collection)

The only regret that the Tecks had on this occasion was that Princess Augusta and her husband were not present. They felt unable to leave Strelitz owing to reports of an epidemic of influenza in England. Princess Augusta was over mindful of her own welfare and could, if she chose, find good excuses to avoid travel. Even so, her presence was much missed but her sister bore no malice for her decision to stay at home.

After the festivities the Tecks decided to spend the summer in England rather than visit Rumpenheim as usual. In the autumn they made a series of visits to the homes of their friends. Wherever they stayed, reports to the press were provided with the names of the guests and in some instances also accounts of the doings of the house party and in particular that of Princess Mary who was always of interest to the public. The Duke and Duchess took enormous pleasure in these large house parties and were very much at their ease with their numerous acquaintances. While never forgetting their rank they managed to be able to be part of society, much more so indeed than other members of the royal family.

H.M. Queen Victoria in 1897 the year of her Diamond Jubilee. This is one of the most famous photographs of the old Queen and was reproduced all over the Empire.
(Photograph by W.D. Downey)

CHAPTER FIVE

Envoi

By the time of her silver wedding anniversary, Princess Mary's children were, with the exception of the youngest, quite grown up. The two elder sons were in the army. Prince Adolphus 'Dolly' was well established, Prince Francis 'Frank' rather less so, because indeed, he was what Victorian parents were apt to call 'unsatisfactory'. He was elegant and stylish, but like his mother, extravagant. However, while he was thought to be a bit 'wild' he had not yet committed any really rash acts to incur parental disapproval. Prince Alexander 'Alge' was still at Eton and was very 'steady'. Princess May was the darling of her father and her mother's devoted companion. Indeed the Princess described her daughter as 'a pearl of great price', her 'Herzblatt'. The young Tecks were all good-looking, charming and agreeable and a great credit to their parents. Everywhere they went everyone spoke of them favourably.

However, there was one difficulty and that was the question of their rank. In England it was not a problem since Queen Victoria had sensibly included her cousin's children as part of the royal family, but on the continent their position was much inferior. At one time, it appears Princess Maud of Wales would have liked to marry Prince Frank, but while he was friendly enough he showed no inclination for anything more. His family might well have wished for the marriage and indeed, when Princess Maud became engaged to Prince Charles of Denmark, Prince Frank's feelings were mixed, but he only had himself to blame for his dilatory behaviour. On another occasion, the Prince of Wales thought Prince Dolly might be a proper husband for one of his daughters. His sister, the Empress Frederick and his mother, Queen Victoria, were not enthusiastic. The tiresome question of rank and position once more loomed large. Indeed, when Prince Dolly did finally marry the charming and attractive Lady Margaret Grosvenor his father was far from pleased. A stout royal princess was what he would have preferred because he was obsessed with the question of rank and position. His youngest son, Alge, did make the sort of marriage his father would have liked. He married Princess Alice of Albany, a most attractive and agreeable person and 'perfectly royal'. This same question was equally important for the future of Princess May. As a Serene Highness there could be no likelihood of a marriage with a German prince of a reigning family even if she were disposed to accept a proposal. However, she had never shown any real inclination to leave England and make her home elsewhere. Indeed, the experience of English princesses in Germany over the years had not been very happy. Moreover, Princess Louise, the fourth daughter of Queen Victoria, had married the Marquess of Lorne and this had been accepted as had the marriage of Princess Louise of Wales to the Duke of Fife. Princess May could quite well marry into the nobility without any real difficulty if she chose.

The Tecks, on the other hand, hoped their children would make brilliant matches; the Duke, in particular, cherished fond hopes of a truly royal alliance but even he in his more rational moments recognized that the possibilities for such were small. However, the chance came when everyone seemed to think that Princess May would do very well for Prince Albert Victor – Eddy as he was called in the family – the elder son of the Prince of Wales. The Princess of Wales had apparently given the project some very real support rather earlier. It would ensure that 'dear Eddy' was not allied to a Prussian and that the Rumpenheim connection would be maintained. Prince Eddy was a charming but rather weak young man who decidedly needed managing. Princess May had a proper upbringing, she had won universal praise in her relationships with her parents and she was totally English in outlook. Prince Eddy led a somewhat dissipated life, he liked pleasure more than work and he was impressionable. He had fallen in love with his cousin, Alice of Hesse, who later married Tsar Nicholas of Russia, but she refused him. He next fancied Princess Hélène of Orleans but she was a Roman Catholic and a marriage to her might cause him to lose his rights of succession under the terms of the Act of Settlement. Nothing came of this romance – apparently Princess Hélène really did love the young man – because of her father's refusal to consider it. Prince Eddy then had several flirtations with other young women, daughters of the aristocracy, but none of these were serious affairs. However, it was clear that he was fickle and did indeed require managing.

Princess Mary's hopes were further enhanced when Princess May was summoned to Balmoral to stay with the Queen. The visit was a great success and upon Princess May's return her mother was effusive in her thanks to her cousin for the hospitality. Plans were then made for the Tecks and their daughter to go to Sandringham but before the visit took place Prince Eddy made his way to Luton Hoo where the Tecks were staying and proposed to Princess May. She accepted him. Princess Mary was delighted as was the country; earlier the Duke of Cambridge had confided to Lady Geraldine Somerset, who incidentally was far from pleased, that the match would be popular with the people. He was quite correct in his assumption. Letters of congratulations poured into White Lodge. Princess Mary was gratified with the universal approbation of the engagement both of the family and the country. She noted to her friend, Lady Salisbury, 'It has been delightful to see the dear Queen's joy at the happy event which fills the hearts of our united families with such intense pleasure and satisfaction, and is a source of so much rejoicing to the nation'. As the Empress Frederick put it most aptly, 'Mary is indeed a lucky person – the one wish of her heart has been fulfilled for her child, and I am sure she is supremely happy'. Other members of the royal family were less enthusiastic. Princess Louise, Marchioness of Lorne was apparently irritated but then she was inclined to be jealous of anyone's happiness, and so was Princess Helena because she wanted her daughter to be the future Princess of Wales. The Duke of Cambridge and his sister, Augusta, were much pleased and Queen Victoria gave a special sign of approbation by noting in the message to the Privy Council that Prince Eddy's fiancée was the daughter of 'H.R.H. Princess Mary'. The year of the engagement passed quickly and the marriage was to take place in February 1892; everyone clamoured to be invited and all of the bride's Rumpenheim connections expected to be included.

The Tecks and their daughter joined the Prince and Princess of Wales at Sandringham for the holidays. Early in January 1892 Prince Eddy caught the influenza, a disease which was very prevalent. His illness became worse, it turned into pneumonia. This caused very real alarm. Princess Mary said in a letter to Lady Salisbury, 'I cannot conceal from you that we are very anxious and must continue so until the crisis is over'. The royal patient did not improve, he soon became delirious, and on 14th January he died surrounded by his parents, two of his sisters, his brother, his fiancée and her parents. All of Princess Mary's hopes were dashed. She wrote to Queen Victoria, 'It seemed *too much, too hard* to bear'!... I am trying to say in all truth and submission: "Thy will be done!"...' The Grand Duchess Augusta in Strelitz wrote to the Duke of Cambridge '...poor Mary! *after all* to come to *this*! no! it is too distressing'. She also wondered on a more practical note who would pay for the expensive trousseau which would not now be needed.

Princess Mary and her family remained for a time at Sandringham and then she and her daughter returned to seclusion at White Lodge. Prince Eddy was buried in St George's Chapel at Windsor. On his grave was a special wreath marked 'Hélène', perhaps symbolic of his true love and certainly a sign of real kindness by the Tecks.

In an effort to make the situation more tolerable, Queen Victoria invited the Tecks and Princess May to Osborne. The aged Queen noted that her cousin's spirits were amazingly good considering the sad state of affairs. After a short sojourn

H.M. King William I of Württemberg was a cousin of Duke Alexander, father of Prince Francis of Teck. He granted Prince Francis the right to be called 'Serene Highness'.
(From the collection of H.M. Queen Beatrix of the Netherlands)

on the Isle of Wight as the Queen's guest, Princess May went to stay at Compton Place with the Prince and Princess of Wales and then returned to White Lodge with her parents.

Meanwhile Princess Mary had prompted her friend, Lady Wolverton, to take a villa in the south of France. For reasons of her own, Princess Mary had wanted to be at Mentône near the Prince of Wales and his family, but the Duke of Cambridge vetoed this plan. It was to Cannes the Teck family would go for a couple of months rest and recuperation from their awful ordeal. In Cannes, Princess Mary cheered up quite quickly. Indeed, on her departure she was to say, 'We were all very sorry to leave that *Paradise* of a place especially with all its *wealth* of *roses* in full *glorious* abundance!' Life in the South of France soon took on the pattern of the Tecks' sojourn in Florence with short expeditions, private dinners and informal gatherings. Everywhere Princess Mary and her daughter were greeted with affection and sympathy.

They had planned to go to Strelitz but for some reason the Grand Duchess put them off, so they went to Württemberg instead where they were the guests of King William and his family. On this occasion they were splendidly housed at the royal residence with their host and hostess nearby. King William was an elegant and charming man, the son of Princess Catherine, but his wife, Queen Charlotte, was very unregal, casual in her appearance and manner which dismayed Princess Mary. However, she and her husband did everything to make their guests feel at ease.

Soon after their arrival, Princess Mary's sitting room caught fire—a lamp ignited the muslin curtains—but fortunately no great damage was done. Princess Mary and her daughter had been frightened because the flames spread rapidly, but the fire brigade extinguished the blaze with only the loss of a few books and several photographs plus the desk on which the lamp had initially been placed. Everyone seems to have regarded the event casually and with some amusement.

As it was now spring, the Württemberg court retired to the country and the Tecks went with them. King William and his consort took up residence in Villa Marienwahl and the Tecks lived in Schloss Ludwigsburg which was an enormous place of some four hundred rooms and in the tradition and style of the eighteenth century. The Tecks were joined by the widowed Duchess of Albany and her two children and they did much to cheer up the whole establishment. The pace of life was unhurried, very informal and domestic with luncheon parties at Marienwahl, walks in the park – the gardens at Ludwigsburg were famous – and expeditions to the country-side and occasionally to Stuttgart itself for the theatre. They even visited the ruins of Teck castle though only a few remnants of it remained, and looked at the view from a sort of tower erected on the site. They took tea in a little room at the top of this curious edifice before returning to the capital of Württemberg. Duke Francis enjoyed being in his native country and liked the deference he received from the local people as well as being fêted by his own regiment, the *Olga Dragooner*.

With the death of Prince Eddy, the matrimonial sweep-stakes were transferred to his brother. The latter had shown some interest in his cousin, Marie, the daughter of the Duke of Edinburgh, but the young princess became engaged to Prince Ferdinand of Roumania. The news of the engagement Princess Mary recorded in her journal, 'Heard of little Marie of Edinburgh's betrothal to the Heir of Roumania, Ferdinand of Hohenzollern, through a telegram from her mother to Queen Olga'. The contents of the telegram cannot but have pleased the Tecks because one more potential bride for the surviving son of the Prince of Wales was removed. Princess Mary was also well aware that 'Aunt Minnie' the Tsarina of Russia, had initially been engaged to the Grand Duke Nicholas but after his death she had ultimately married his younger brother, later Tsar Alexander III. The possibility of Princess May marrying Prince George was not inconceivable.

This continental tour ended in early July and the family life at White Lodge was almost as if the ill fated engagement had never happened. All three of Princess Mary's sons were now in the army, the youngest was at Sandhurst and the elder two serving officers. Princess May resumed the role of companion to her mother and occupied herself with the latter's numerous charities. The family were still in half-mourning so many of the usual social activities were curtailed.

There was a custom among royal families in particular to retain the apartments of the deceased precisely as they were at the time of an individual's demise. Indeed, sometimes whole palaces were virtually abandoned and only visited on the occasion of the melancholy anniversary. Prince Albert's bedroom and dressing room were never occupied after December 1861 and it was said that every night his valet continued to bring hot water and to lay out his evening clothes. In Russia, the Pavlovski Palace, the home of the widow of Tsar Paul, became a shrine after her death in 1825 and in Berlin visitors were shown the rooms once used by King Frederick William IV. Princess Victoria, the eldest daughter of Queen Victoria, remarks at various times about these and similar rooms and their lugubrious effect on the guests.

'The awful day,' that is, the 14th December, was always commemorated by the Queen and her family with church services and a visit to Frogmore. The Prince and Princess of Wales while less morbid than the Queen had kept Prince Eddy's room just as it was on the day of his death. The Tecks and Princess May went to Sandringham in December for a few days and then back to White Lodge for Christmas. Princess Mary never allowed herself to be despondent for long and was bustling about with her family. Her three sons, daughter, husband and brother and the household had the usual trees and as always there was a great collection of presents. The celebrations were not quite as gay as in the past but they were not melancholy.

Visits to country houses were very much part of Princess Mary's life and she felt that they could be resumed, albeit on a limited scale, when she accepted the invitation of the Duke of Newcastle to stay at Clumber. The house party was not a large one: the host and hostess, Lord Latham, Lady Albertha Wilbraham, Lord and Lady Churchill, Mr Arthur and Lady

H.R.H. Prince George of Wales, Duke of York the son-in-law of Princess Mary.
(From the Review of Reviews — private collection)

Clementina Walsh, Lady Irene Hastings and Miss Mary Thesiger as well as the Tecks, their daughter and youngest son. The elder boys had rejoined their regiments. Clumber was the sort of household Princess Mary much enjoyed. It was grand and well run, the royals had nice sets of rooms with good servants, there was an endless round of social activities, short walks on fine days, drives in open landaus, dinners, music and whist in the evening and sometimes dancing. Princess Mary partook of all of these in varying degrees. After Clumber, the Tecks and Princess May moved on to Windsor where it was evident that the latter was very much on the minds of the aged Queen and her eldest daughter who was visiting. The newspapers constantly speculated on potential brides for Prince George and inevitably returned to Princess May. The German Empress had mixed feelings about the latter, sometimes totally approving and sometimes filled with doubts. The doubts were because she felt the Tecks' daughter was not overly spiritual or intellectual but while having her reservations she always really believed Princess May was the right wife for her nephew: 'She made a very nice impression on me!' and 'she is a good steady girl I am sure and will always do her duty'. All of this speculation and comment must have been a real strain on everyone, Princess Mary, the anxious mother; Princess May, the possible bride; and Prince George, the uncertain suitor.

The matter was resolved when Princess May was able to tell her joyful parents early in May that Prince George had proposed and that she had accepted him. Princess Mary sent off the happy news to all and sundry. The public were pleased and as the Duke of Cambridge had earlier observed quite correctly that such a solution would be liked. He was delighted to have his opinion confirmed. Dozens of telegrams and letters began to flow into White Lodge and the wedding day was set for July. Queen Victoria who did not care much for weddings: 'melancholy things' she called them and disapproved of long engagements which were 'very trying and not very good'. Princess Mary was relieved to have the matter settled but further she was agreeably surprised considering the known stinginess of her elder sister when the latter and her husband were willing to pay for the new trousseau. The bride's mother declared, 'I am determined that all the silk shall come from England, all the flannel from Wales, all the tweeds from Scotland, and every yard of lace and poplin from Ireland.' Princess Mary was in her element supervising everything; there was a constant bustle at White Lodge; 'on one side... was a pile of telegrams received... on the other... were packets of telegraph forms. Messages were constantly being delivered...' and everyone helped draft replies. Every day there were visits to the Imperial Institute to view the magnificent wedding presents. The bridal dress was woven in England with the traditional roses, thistles and shamrocks in the silk brocade. *Maiblumen* which had featured so much in the first engagement did not reappear. Much to the delight of Princess Mary, her daughter wished to wear the same simple bridal veil of her mother. Although this wedding was a grand affair, the bridal veil could serve to symbolize the rather simple ceremony at Kew Church over two decades earlier and the real domestic happiness that had been enjoyed by the Tecks. This time the ceremony would take place in the Chapel Royal in St James's Palace and much to the delight of Princess Mary who liked to reinforce her relationship with 'the old royal family' because it was here that her grandparents, George III and Charlotte of Mecklenburg, had been married over a century earlier.

Two days before the wedding Princess Mary, her husband and daughter moved from White Lodge to Buckingham Palace. The grandeur of the royal residence in the capital of the Empire suited Princess Mary precisely. The Duke of Teck also revelled in the situation in which he found himself. Indeed, his constant concern for rank and precedence might at long last be said to have found its response. His only daughter, a mere serene highness, was to become the wife of the future king of England. A delicious irony for one who had felt snubbed by minor princelings in Germany.

Princess Mary accompanied the Queen in the procession to the Chapel Royal. She quite overwhelmed her cousin, not only by her size but by her enthusiastic response to the crowd. By an accident, and contrary to precedence, the sovereign and Princess Mary arrived rather earlier than expected. To resolve the dilemma the latter proposed that the former retire to a nearby sitting room. Princess Mary, on the other hand, fully intended to take her own place immediately to be able to enjoy the spectacle when Queen Victoria abruptly altered everything by preceding her cousin and taking her seat with the result that the bride's mother and groom's grandmother were all ensconced when the guests reached the chapel. This was the only hitch in the whole grand affair. The splendid portrait by Tuxen illustrates the scene most graphically and indeed, Princess Mary in the right foreground is a dominant figure. Lady Geraldine Somerset aptly described Princess Mary's elation. 'Will her head be still on her shoulders tomorrow! – I believe it will have expanded and blown to the moon!!'

The reception was held at Buckingham Palace. A great gaggle of royal relations were present, the elated and triumphant parents, her three brothers, her beloved Aunt Augusta Strelitz and her blind husband the Grand Duke, her uncle the Duke of Cambridge and many cousins who had frequented the halls of Rumpenheim. As for the groom's parents, the Prince of Wales looked grand and the Princess pale and wan but ethereal in white satin. To quote Lady Geraldine, she 'looked *more lovely* – than ever – more can approach her!' George's sisters and his cousins were there. Several of the princesses were probably much aggrieved not to have been the bride. The groom's aged Danish grandparents, the King and Queen of Denmark, were another Rumpenheim link. This was the world which Princess Mary relished and understood, a gathering of family to witness a marriage that was not only the culmination of her own dreams and plans but brought together in England all who meant so much to her personally.

To symbolize the event forever, the Tecks joined the

Princess Mary and her daughter at the time of the latter's engagement to Prince George of Wales, Duke of York.
(From a private collection)

Queen on the central balcony of Buckingham Palace to see th
bridal party depart. Nobody could regard them as inferior
ever again. The Tecks were in tears of joy and of sadness
firstly because they realized their beloved only daughter ha
reached the pinnacle to which they had aspired and neve
attained, and secondly because they knew that they would b
very lonely without her. Indeed, if the old Duchess of Cam
bridge had so much relied on Princess Mary for compan
ionship, the latter had come to do the same with her daughter
Queen Victoria put it most precisely, 'What Mary will d
without May, I cannot think for she is her right hand.'

  With the ceremonies at an end, the guests and crow
dispersed. The Tecks had a simple tea and then went for
drive. Life had to be picked up anew after these few days o
magic. Although like most Victorian parents the Tecks wep
at their daughter's leave-taking, they soon regained thei
spirits and once more ensconced in White Lodge they re
sumed their normal existence. The numerous charitable acti
vities now loomed larger and larger on Princess Mary's exist
ence. The visits to various institutions continued, there wer
prizes to be awarded—indeed she was quite professional at thi
occupation and being essentially a kind and generous indi
vidual, she usually had just the right remark for the happ
recipient—garden fêtes and bazaars to be attended, patients i
hospitals to be visited and her special enthusiasm, the Needle
work Guild, of which she was not only patroness but als
president required her close attention. In the year of he
daughter's marriage, the Guild collected some 22,000 item
for distribution to 'the deserving poor'. The Princess was no
merely a symbolic head of the Guild, she was very directl
involved, admonishing, directing and encouraging. In a lette
to the ladies of the Surrey branch she noted 'the kind of article
sent has been much better, the material being of a mor
serviceable nature' and pointed out 'the spirit of the Guil
should be more thoroughly understood... the main object..
is to help those most in need.... I would remind all that th
Guild is not religious work.... We all work for our poore

rethren, and that our gifts are for Church people, Dissenters, Roman Catholics, Jews, or indeed any who need help.' These interests were to sustain her in part in coping with the ailing Duke of Teck but without the support of her daughter, life at White Lodge was not to be easy.

The bustle and activity of the wedding had quite exhausted Princess Mary, much as she had enjoyed them. The family were certain that she was un-well and they were all convinced that a complete rest was required and, therefore, a sojourn first in Neuenahr and a long stay in St Moritz was proposed. Princess Mary agreed and she and her youngest son, Prince Alge, left England in the early summer of 1893. Just before leaving they were told that the Duke of Teck's sister, Amelia Countess von Hügel, had died. The Duke was much affected by this melancholy news but his wife was rather less so. She and her sisters-in-law had been on amiable enough terms but they were never close. However, it did mean that the household was plunged into black and it cast a pall over the projected continental holiday.

Never one to allow gloomy events to become overly dominant in her life, Princess Mary cast aside the melancholy ambiance of White Lodge quite quickly and was determined to enjoy her vacation. Aside from the distressed state of mind of the Duke of Teck, the start was not auspicious, the train almost left without the luggage and the servants and the Channel crossing was initially unpleasant. Once on land, things improved considerably, the compartments in the train were commodious and 'It was a most perfect day for traveling,' Princess Mary wrote to a friend, 'as the heavy rain had effectually laid the dust, the air was cool and pleasant and the sun not overpowering.' However, as the school holidays were starting the trains all ran very late. Upon arrival at her destination, Princess Mary was much relieved for she recognized that she really did require a proper rest. Neuenahr was nothing more than the name of the hotal site where she was to take the waters, but nearby were two pleasant villages for the usual expeditions.

H.I.M. William II, the German Emperor, in one of his many fancy costumes. Here, he is dressed as the Protector of the Johanniter Order. Princess Mary quite liked him and he always made an effort to be agreeable to the Tecks. (From a private collection)

Princess Mary's travel impedimenta consisted not merely of the usual luggage but of personal items such as books, bibelots and photographs to make her rooms more *gemütlich*. Virtually the first thing she did on arrival on this occasion, as on the previous sojourns in similar establishments, was to rearrange the furniture to her liking – the Duke of Teck's spirit, not his actual presence, was being felt – and set up her personal photographs. After a fortnight of taking the cure in a mild sort of way, visiting the local sights and paying calls on relations; for example, she went to Bonn to see Princess Victoria of Schaumburg-Lippe, the daughter of the Empress Frederick and described by Princess Mary as 'a great dear and enchantingly English' – not a recommendation to certain circles in Berlin, probably. The royal party went to St Moritz. Once more the routine of the past was resumed and, indeed, life at St Moritz was in many ways an extension of life at White Lodge. There was a plethora of visiting royals and aristocrats to provide satisfactory company and the usual round of calls to provide a diversion. The stay in Switzerland was agreeable enough but Princess Mary found that she much missed the company of her daughter, who 'had always been the life of our little party,' and that she had 'hoped everything from St Moritz, but was sadly disappointed'. Two family visits completed the summer tour, one with Princess Catherine of Württemberg at Villa Seefeld 'a delightful pretty, quiet place, and a perfect retreat for any one wanting peace and rest'. At this rustic retreat Princess Mary and her hostess were joined by Prince Francis – the latter was still very much the object of the Württemberg princess's affection – for a few days. The second visit was with the King and Queen of Württemberg, where they were to stay at Ludwigsburg for five days. The same pattern of life as in the past occurred with dinners, receptions, soirées and expeditions.

After being away for over four months, the Tecks were happy to be ensconced in their own home. Moreover, they had a new occupation, namely helping their daughter to furnish York House. The young couple had been given that

Princess Mary accompanied by her daughter on a visit to a factory making silk cloth. The Princess was much interested in the promotion of British industry and incidentally in the welfare of the workers and their families.
(From the biography of Princess Mary by C. Kinloch Cooke, published in 1900 — Courtesy John Murray)

Schloss Rumpenheim in Germany, the favourite summer holiday home of the Cambridge and Hesse families. Rumpenheim was not entirely approved of by Queen Victoria, who suspected it to be the centre of anti-Prussian feelings. In this she was right. Schloss Rumpenheim was destroyed in World War II.
(From a copy in a private collection)

ection of St James's Palace formerly occupied by the Duchess
of Cambridge. Ironically, for a brief time it had been set up as
a bachelor establishment for Princess May's late fiancée,
Prince Eddy. With the family's strong sense of history, this
was vastly pleasing to everyone. There was one difficulty in
that Princess Mary rather tended to use York House as a *pied à
terre* in London. She and her husband were to lunch and dine
here frequently, rather too frequently for the Duke of York
who found Princess Mary's casual attitudes about punctuality
very irritating. He had put up with his mother's dilatory
habits when he was at home but he did not intend to allow his
mother-in-law to assume a similar role in his own house. The
Duke of Teck was filled with ideas about how York House
should be decorated and many hours were consumed in making sketches and visiting shops for Princess Mary and her
husband vastly missed their daughter's company and in many
ways were rather at a loose end.

The Yorks appreciated the general situation and tried to be
kind, but they had their own lives and their own interests. To
some degree the myriad charities did provide a very real
activity anew but without her daughter, Princess Mary felt
very limited. She did try and persuade the Yorks to help, but
while the numerous charitable activities loomed large on
Princess Mary's horizon, they were small on the large scene of
the Duke and Duchess of York. The latter were mildly co-
operative but they could not bind themselves to preside at
dinners, bazaars and the like. One new activity was a very
close involvement with the affairs of the 'National Silk
Association of Great Britain and Ireland'; this body was
founded in 1887 to promote the somewhat depressed silk
trade and Princess Mary was energetic in getting her coterie of
ladies to support it. Indeed, so successful was she in promoting this cause that a very large exhibition of the products of the
silk weavers was arranged to take place at Stafford House in
the spring of 1894. Unfortunately, as a result of her heavy
involvement in this project and her usually busy social round,
Princess Mary became exhausted and all of the good that had

come from the continental holiday was lost.

The Yorks invited Princess Mary to come to them a Sandringham. 'York Cottage' was an inadequate house that had been designed by Colonel Edis; it had few good rooms and it was furnished in a very unimaginative way with almost everything from Maples and an essentially middle class and boring lack of style. Everything had been arranged by the Duke of York, his mother and sisters before his marriage, his fiancée's good taste was not considered. However, Princess Mary, unlike her daughter, thought it delightful. In a letter written to Mary Thesiger in December 1893 she said, 'This is the perfection of an ideal cottage; each room is charming in its own way, and everything in perfect taste and most cosy and comfortable'. Moreover, it was so convenient to 'The Big House', satisfactory to Princess Mary for frequent visits to the Wales's but she, never much liking being alone, could not appreciate that for a young couple to be cheek-by-jowl with the parents-in-law might not always be quite satisfactory. Princess Augusta was more perceptive noting that the Yorks 'had far better have their own Entourage and friends'. Princess Mary would not have understood such sentiments. Of course, her sister had lived in close proximity to her parents-in-law and knew exactly of which she spoke. The Wales's were kind and Princess Mary during her stay noted in letters and in her journal dining at Sandringham with all of the family much to her delight. She passionately revelled in the house-party ambiance and this was very much maintained by the Prince of Wales and his wife.

By Christmas 1894, all the royal family were aware that the Duchess of York was pregnant. The prospect of being the grandmother to an heir to the British throne filled Princess Mary with great excitement. She fussed over her daughter, visited her constantly and gave much unsolicited advice. Of course the event was important but it loomed much larger to Princess Mary and her husband. The latter, who was more fidgety and difficult, was even more satisfied with his daughter's position and future and his own as grandfather to a future king-emperor. It almost consoled him for his own lack of royal rank. Princess Mary did not neglect her charities in her anxiety and concern about her daughter's well being. As usual she used all her powers of persuasion to get help from her aristocratic acquaintances and to promote meetings. She did not hesitate to work on her royal relations as well. The widowed Duchess of Albany with whom she was on very good terms was constantly being asked to grace meetings to bring out loyal supporters. Friends were asked to 'get up a theatrical performance... to clear off... a part of the debt' for some favoured charity and in April she thought that she should have no hesitation in asking Mr Irving to give... a Matinee'. At the same time, full preparations were being made for the silk exhibition, letters were despatched to distinguished patrons and political figures to assist. The Lord Lieutenant of Ireland was requested to use his 'best endeavours to persuade the manufacturers' with an interest in the trade 'to exhibit some of their lovely stuffs on the occasion'. Were they to do so everyone would benefit. Even the Duchess of Sutherland who had kindly offered the loan of Stafford House for the affair was cajoled into allowing more space for 'a most interesting and valuable contribution from India'. Princess Mary was indefatigable and most persuasive and nobody could resist her when she was determined in a plan of action for her charities. Princess Mary was able to record her pleasure at the satisfactory result of everyone's combined efforts when she wrote to Lady Salisbury, 'You will rejoice to hear that our Silk Exhibition has been a thorough success, and is already bearing fruit, as evidenced by some of the shops most opposed to the movement now advertising 'English Silks"'.

All these charitable and social activities were but a diversion and were placed in their more limited perspective when it was decided that the Duchess of York should go to White Lodge where the royal infant would be born. Princess Mary was enchanted and had her beloved daughter under her own roof once more; Princess May was 'home' with her mother.

On 23rd June 1894, the long awaited event occurred
Princess Mary was a grandmother and her grandson would
ultimately be king. Telegrams were despatched to all and
sundry; indeed, the sending of telegrams seems to have been a
royal avocation. 'The royal mob' responded with alacrity and
the Duchess of Teck's household was kept busy keeping note
of the names of those who sent their best wishes. Princess
Mary also received her cousin, the Queen, who came to call
and on this occasion one could say that 'the old royal family'
and 'the royal family' were truly united. The christening
ceremony saw this feeling renewed in a very real sense and the
little boy the symbol of the union of the two traditions. It was
Rumpenheim and Coburg combined. However, it had not
been easy at White Lodge as the Duke of York was to observe
later of his situation. 'I wouldn't go through the six weeks
spent at White Lodge for anything she [Princess Mary] used to
come in and disturb us and then her unpunctuality used to
annoy me too dreadfully.' He recognized it was all meant
kindly but it was very trying. An escape from the parents-in-
law was for him a necessity.

Early in August, Princess Mary, Prince Francis, their
daughter – very dutifully and a bit reluctantly – and youngest
son, left England for St Moritz. As her comptroller noted, she
'derived great pleasure from her visits and the quiet weeks
passed in the Engandine... not only gave her renewed health
and strength, but an entire freedom from all ceremonial etiquette'. The Duke of Teck and his son left them at the Hotel
Victoria. He intended to make his usual visits to Württemberg
relations. And once more Princess Mary arranged her quarters to her liking with 'stuffs, cushions and photographs,'
without which she never travelled and the result being 'a most
cosy snug'. Various royal relations and friends were staying in
and around St Moritz. As usual the ubiquitous Vera Württemberg and her unmarried daughters were very much in
evidence but so too were Elizabeth of Hesse-Anhalt and Princess Mary's cousin, Helene Mecklenburg-Altenburg – described by Princess Mary as 'greatly aged and altered' but

*The Duke and Duchess of Teck and the Prince and Princess of Wales — a domestic scene of about 1890.
(From The Illustrated London News)*

considering they had not met for eighteen years this coul⟨
have been hardly surprising. As Princess May was to not⟨
rather tactfully in a letter to her eldest brother of these an⟨
other 'royals' that it was 'quite a cousinly gathering!' Th⟨
pleasures on this occasion were simple: walks, expeditions
luncheons '*coffee'd* in a covered arbor', and musical evenings
On one tour there was an accident. Princess Mary wrote in he⟨
journal, 'Our horse shied close by the bridge at a load of ha⟨
lying by the road and turned around, and, but for Hood'⟨
quickness and presence of mind, we might have been upse⟨
into the river'. Nelson Hood commended the princess'⟨
equanimity observing that she 'was calm and collected, no⟨
showing any fear'. All in all it was a delightful three week⟨
concluding with a short trip to Württemberg, Princess Ma⟨
having left before this part of the trip was made. Princes⟨
Mary was now rested and ready for her next major socia⟨
appearance, namely, the wedding of her eldest son. Princes⟨
Mary said of herself at this time, 'St Moritz, as usual, ha⟨
worked wonders for me, and I am told I am looking, and I an⟨
most certainly feeling (*unberufen*) particularly *well and fresh*⟨
I only hope the *wear* and *tear* of my daily life... will not und⟨
all the good effects of the holiday.' It is evident that Princes⟨
Mary was almost as addicted to underlinings as her cousin th⟨
Queen.

The wedding of Prince Dolly was to take place on 27t⟨
November and the autumn was passed agreeably in the man⟨
preparations. In addition, the infant grandson, Prince Edwar⟨
of York, was a delightful diversion and, like most dotin⟨
grandmothers, Princess Mary thought him perfection. Sh⟨
called him 'my darling', 'extraordinarily precocious' an⟨
'really a remarkably fine child!' Indeed she was almost overl⟨
possessive about him since he had been born under her roo⟨
and lived at White Lodge the first few weeks of his life saying,⟨
'I have come to look upon him as almost my *very own*!'

The death of Tsar Alexander III caused no change of plan⟨
for the wedding despite the fact that he was the Princess o⟨
Wales's brother-in-law but that of Princess Claudine of Teck⟨

id. She had been predeceased a year earlier by her sister, rincess Amelia, so the Duke of Teck was the last of his eneration. Of course, he attended his sister's funeral. His oungest son, Prince Alge, went with him. The whole business was more than usually lugubrious since the Princess Claudine had diphtheria and her house had to be fumigated nd the funeral carriages and hearse made a short and direct xcursion rather than the traditional cortege through Graz as vould have been customary. When the wedding did finally ccur on 12th December it was a very great event as the Westminsters were vastly wealthy–the Duke was reckoned to e the richest peer and the biggest private landowner in England. Prince Dolly, all were agreed, was charming; only the Duke of Teck was inclined to be less than happy since his daughter-in-law was not of royal blood–yet another foolish xample of his concern for rank and position. All of Princess Mary's friends had given splendid wedding gifts which enured that the wealth of the bride's family did not outshine the omewhat impoverished state of that of the groom.

A break in the family circle occurred when Prince Alge vas ordered to join his regiment in India and would go with it rom there to the Cape Colony. It was expected that he would e away for three years, no longer so readily available to ccompany his parents on their continental expeditions and to help enliven the somewhat melancholy household at White Lodge. Their son-in-law and daughter did what they could to cheer things up but they had their own busy lives with many official duties to be performed. Once again it was a round of house parties and the inevitable charities that kept Princess Mary reasonably content. The inundation of articles for the London Needle Work Guild continued apace. At the end of he year Princess Mary wrote that she was sending numerous articles, sorted and tied up in fives with red ribbon; also two arge bales containing 486 articles... not opened'. Further tems were to be sent later – a very real example of her own personal involvement. Her enthusiastic support for the many good causes brought to her attention had its own reward.

H.R.H. Princess Dagmar of Denmark. Empress of Russia after her marriage, her great wealth and power contrasted markedly with the modest establishment of the Teck family. Yet this rich cousin always treated them with great affection. (From the collection of H.M. The Queen of Denmark, Royal Library, Copenhagen)

Commenting how well she had always been received by the public she said on one occasion, 'During the time of the riots in London I drove about as usual, and was never molested in any way. I have invariably met with courtesy from the people, and cannot speak too highly of them.'

The spring of 1895 saw legions of royal visitors to enjoy the splendours of the London season. At Ascot for example 20 *royalties* filling five carriages' and to highlight it all the Prince of Wales won with his horse *Persimmon*. This was the world which Princess Mary found to her liking and it helped to distract her from her increasingly unstable husband and the absence of her children. One of the latter's activities did not please. Prince Frank, her favourite son, got into a terrible scrape losing ten thousand pounds on a bet at the races. The family rescued him, the Tecks themselves paying half the sum despite their strained finances. Prince Frank was 'exiled' to India.

Possibly because of the precarious state of the Teck household with respect to ready money – Prince Frank having required all that was available – there was no continental holiday. A more modest plan was adopted in an excursion to Scotland which the Tecks had not visited for some years. They were not to be the Queen's guests at Balmoral but to make an informal sojourn based at the hotel at Strathpeffer.

As at St Moritz, Princess Mary's rooms were rearranged to her own taste, the furniture moved about and the bibelots and family photographs put in place. Scotland in August while very attractive with the heather does not necessarily have the best weather. Almost every day Princess Mary recorded, 'Alas! it came on to pour with rain'. Undeterred, the days passed with highland walks, luncheons, teas and dinners with friends. All the gentry and their tenants gave Princess Mary and her husband a great welcome with pipers, flags and children plus the inevitable bouquets of flowers. These expeditions, simple in themselves, gave Princess Mary the feeling she was very much part of the country. A note in her journal for 11th September summed up her sentiments. 'Left about six, highly pleased with our visit, and drove back the same way, partly in rain.' The royal party moved on to Hopetoun and while there made several trips into Edinburgh. One was somewhat melancholy, it being a troop review at which the Duke of Cambridge presided – 'his last review as Commander-in-Chief'. The world was changing and the principal actors on the stage were growing increasingly old.

On 14th December the Tecks became grandparents for the second time. On this occasion the baby was not born at White Lodge but in London. The infant's birth coincided with the anniversary of the death of the Prince Consort much to the consternation of all and naturally he was called Albert after his great grandfather. Princess Mary privately hoped that his last name, George, might 'some day... supplant the *less favoured* one!' The baby was called Bertie by his family but ironically George did finally supplant 'the less *favoured* one' in 1936 when he succeeded to the throne. Indeed, his elder brother who had been christened Edward after 'dear Eddy', whose real name was, of course, Albert Victor, was known to his relations as David, and Edward was only used officially until he became Prince of Wales and later upon his succession as Edward VIII.

Princess Mary's health now began to fail. Her son, Frank, wrote from 'exile' in India, 'All your friends tell me you don't look well – so you must take care of yourself... tell your charitable friends to "go to hell." Say this once in a loud voice and the only bother you'll have is to hear from them no more'. She actually began to comply with such advice and curtailed some of her activities but she did not find it easy to do so. A holiday at St Moritz and Bad Nauheim with her daughter the following summer did effect some improvement but, as she wrote to the Bishop of Stepney, 'I still feel the need of *rest* and care'. This was to be her last continental holiday and before she returned to England she made a short side-trip to Rumpenheim. It still had all of its charm for her and was filled with souvenirs of the past. As Prince Frank was to say to his mother, 'Your visit... must have conjured up a varied assort-

H.R.H. Prince Albert always regarded Princess Mary with affection. He was much interested in her welfare and happiness and played a very real role in the search for a suitable husband.
(From the collection of H.M. The Queen — photograph by B.E. Dupper)

ment of recollections and as… you visited every room… one might say a death or birth in every bedroom'. All was totally unchanged and hence absolutely delightful – nostalgia coloured all memories.

Upon her return people noted her general lack of energy and less healthy appearance. While staying at Warfield Park she suffered some sort of attack which seriously alarmed her and she observed to a friend, 'I don't want to die yet, I cannot leave my children – my sons want me still.' When her family received the news of her illness they were much concerned and immediately they all advised her to rest and to abandon some of her multifarious activities. To ensure that she was not overly persuaded to busy herself too much with her numerous charitable concerns her daughter proposed a stay at York Cottage for some weeks. Once more there were pleasant evenings *en famille* and dinners with the Wales's at Sandringham where a sizeable house party had been gathered for the shooting. Such society delighted Princess Mary and she seemed to have totally recovered from her indisposition of the early autumn. She was able to go back to White Lodge for the Christmas activities but the party was smaller than in the past and the two younger Teck princes were abroad with their regiments. The Duke was an added problem as he was evidently already exhibiting signs of instability which was ultimately to be the course of his complete withdrawal from society after his wife's death. His memory was more uncertain, his irascibility more obvious and his rages more violent. The Empress Frederick thought him 'to have softening of the brain'. Obviously he was suffering from a series of slight strokes which caused his difficulties and made him far from easy.

In the spring of 1897 Princess Mary had to have a major operation for a strangulated hernia but she made a very rapid recovery much to the surprise and delight of everyone and she wrote that she was 'taking roast lamb and mint sauce, boiled mutton, roast chicken, asparagus, spinach … and every kind of jelly!' This was not the diet of an invalid. Her prowess was aided by the fact that her youngest son was on his way home from the Cape Colony and she came downstairs on his return. She had herself ensconced in a chair in the entrance hall in White Lodge so he would see her as soon as he entered the house. All of her many friends had rallied during her illness and there were legions of letters and messages as well as bouquets of flowers arriving almost every day. All of this attention cheered Princess Mary and undoubtedly had their effect on her spirits and general well being.

More importantly, perhaps, was her concern to be well enough to attend the festivities surrounding her cousin's jubilee. She made her London headquarters at Prince Dolly's house which spared her the journey from White Lodge. London was filled with visitors and numerous royal relations flocked to London for the occasion. Indeed Empress Frederick described Buckingham Palace as 'like a beehive'. Princess Mary's sister had even come over from Strelitz although she had many reservations about the arrangements and, in particular, the service outside St Paul's, observing that it was thanking 'God in the Street!!!' Princess Mary revelled in the celebrations and attended everything. At the special garden party she was in a bath-chair but was very much the centre of a coterie of friends. She also chose to attend the fancy dress ball at Devonshire House as the Electress Sophia although she did not take any part in the dancing.

The members of the public, who regarded 'Fat Mary' with great affection, were able to show their feelings and sentiments when she appeared in the royal procession. Indeed, after the Queen herself, the people cheered most loudly for her and this was especially true when the carriages were greeted by the ordinary citizens. Princess Mary was much affected by her reception and was determined to reciprocate in the only way she could by laying the cornerstone at a new isolation hospital for Richmond and Isleworth at Mogden. She delighted the crowd when she said to the Mayor of Richmond that after a quarter of a century of effort, the hospital was now a reality as it proved to them that she had

See facing page

202

H.R.H. Princess Alexandra, Princess of Wales, shown here in two versions, in youth and maturity, as Princess, and, later, as Queen. She was the eldest daughter of King Christian IX of Denmark and was, like Princess Mary, distinctly anti-Prussian. She was a fond and faithful friend of the Teck family.
(Alexandra as Queen from Review of Reviews, private collection, and as Princess from the collection of H.M. the Queen of Denmark, Royal Library, Copenhagen)

really known of the community's problems in the past trying to get a proper isolation hospital. It was acts of this nature that endeared the princess to the public since she never seemed remote from the problems of ordinary people.

While Princess May was well married, as was Prince Dolly and consequently settled, the younger sons were still part of the household. Prince Frank, back from India, now wanted to go to Egypt. His behaviour was not altogether satisfactory and his involvement with a woman whom the family did not approve of did not make the situation better. Ostensibly Prince Frank wanted active service, which he succeeded in obtaining, but his parents constantly worried about him and his extravagant ways. Prince Alge was 'very steady' and a great comfort. To recuperate from the Jubilee celebrations, the Tecks accepted an invitation to stay at Belford Hall near Berwick. Princess Mary recognized that she was still far from well observing to her old friend, Mrs Dalrymple, 'I have no pain now but often discomfort and a great feeling of weariness'. The bracing air, it was hoped, might effect a more permanent cure but it could only be done if she totally abandoned all thoughts of any public duties which she was loath to do.

Prior to her departure to Berwick, Princess Mary had her grandchildren to stay with her at White Lodge. She spoiled the two little boys – the elder nearly three and the younger not quite two – and cosseted the baby girl. When they departed she was very sad that the 'darling chicks left us yesterday, and the house feels most desolate'.

The royal party – Princess Mary, her husband and youngest son – took up residence at the end of August. The entire domestic staff of White Lodge accompanied them – some sixteen in all – as well as a nurse. Prince Alge's presence provided a very real support to his mother in dealing with her husband's instability. Prince Alge was a cheerful companion and helped make the settling in relatively easy. Once a routine was established he felt he could leave his parents and much to his mother's delight he was asked to Osborne for a few days.

Apparently the old Queen found him charming company. His mother said to her second son of his young brother, '*He was much made of*'–high praise indeed.

Belford Hall was a large house built about 1755 and it was furnished with items that came from their hostess's aunt's palazzo in Naples. The gardens were substantial and provided agreeable walks for the invalid and her companions. In addition, there were the usual excursions to visit the neighbouring 'places' inhabited by friends and acquaintances. Indeed, the stay at Berwick was apparently a great success and she was able to say to a friend, 'I am beginning to feel my old strong self again albeit still kept in a way to invalid habits'. The six weeks' sojourn in the bracing climate and relaxed society convinced everyone that all was well.

Once back at White Lodge, Princess Mary was busy with the London Needlework Guild affairs. There were the usual parcels to be packed and the correspondence with the numerous volunteers required her attention. To assist in these efforts, Princess May came to stay for a few days. The latter noted that her mother, despite the recent holiday in the north and the sojourn with the Mount Stephens, was not really well. However, the Duchess of Teck could not be deflected from her activities and also planned a small dinner party to divert her daughter. Nobody thought that there was anything seriously wrong, only a lassitude and weakness and no change of plans was considered. The Duke and his youngest son went off to the theatre but his wife did not accompany them, remaining at home with her daughter, pleased to have her company alone and to hear about the Irish tour.

The end came quite suddenly. Princess Mary was visibly unwell on the Tuesday 26th October. An emergency operation was determined on; the problem was, as before, a strangulated hernia; however, the patient was calm and initially all was satisfactory but shortly thereafter she relapsed and died early in the morning. The cause of death being 'weakness of heart'. Her husband, daughter and youngest son were at the bedside. Prince Frank was in Egypt and Prince

Dolly was staying with his parents-in-law and was only informed of the operation after his mother had died.

The family was stunned and dozens of cards and messages of sympathy were sent. Princess Mary, although she had made no will, had expressed a wish to be buried at Windsor. Her daughter in a letter to Queen Victoria said, 'She particularly disliked the idea of being buried in the damp vault at Kew in spite of her parents being buried there.' Her husband collapsed, his daughter Princess Mary the Duchess of York observed to her Aunt Augusta in Neu-Strelitz, 'For Papa it is cruel and his sad state makes it so much worse, he was so despondent... and God knows what he will do.' He lingered for three years, increasingly mentally unstable and totally absent from public view, and was to be buried beside his wife at Windsor.

With the Victorian interest in funerals, all was as Princess Mary would have liked. The ladies of the household stayed with the coffin until it left White Lodge. On the bier among the floral tributes was a wreath brought by two children from one of the many orphanages that had been the recipient of Princess Mary's concerns.

While one is not on oath in writing lapidary inscriptions, as Dr Johnson once said, *The Times* leader contained a number of very apt and perceptive comments about the deceased, all of which would have pleased her. The writer noted that Princess Mary was 'beloved by the British people and better known than some in a more exalted position', that 'the inborn geniality of the Princess Mary would have won her a place of her own in the hearts of her country men and country women, even if she had not devoted herself from an early age to works of charity and beneficence.' Finally, 'Indeed she always undertook a larger share of public duties than she could fairly have been charged with, and when it is considered that she only had a grant of £5,000 from Parliament, it must be acknowledged that she did all in her power to fulfil her obligations to the community in which her lot was cast.'

The funeral ceremonies were attended by a vast concourse

f people. Her sister and brother-in-law, both elderly, did not ttend but almost all other royal relations were present. The Queen was represented by her eldest son – the only funeral she ctually attended was that of her aunt, the Duchess of Cambridge. Members of the aristocracy were the pallbearers. This was fitting since Princess Mary had mixed so freely. Many rdinary citizens sent flowers and in the East End of London lmost every woman put on crepe. It proved that she was ffectionately regarded by those whom she had helped with er many charities. Her life could be summed up in her own vords. On one occasion she said, 'I have not much money to ive away, but what I have, time, money and influence I give ladly' and at another time, 'I am here to do a little good, and I vill do it while I can.' She was very much 'the People's 'rincess'. The mob knew her as 'Fat Mary' and she did much o make monarchy popular. She was unique for her day in that he was never remote. Nevertheless, she was always concious of her rank and position – her remark as a child, 'I am 'rincess Mary Adelaide of Great Britain' – was something she .ever forgot, but unlike many of her contemporaries in a imilar position she was at ease in general society. For she enuinely liked people. Not for her was the exclusiveness of nany of 'the royal mob', and in being herself on all occasions – npunctual, generous-spirited, gay and thoroughly easy, she arned and enjoyed the affection of almost everyone. She was tot perfect but she was engaging and it was this that gave olour and style to her existence.

SELECTED BIBLIOGRAPHY

Balfour, Michael, *The Kaiser & His Times* (1965).

Bamford, Francis and Wellington, The Duke of (eds.), *The Journal of Mrs Arbuthnot 1820-1832* (1950).

Battiscombe, Georgina, *Queen Alexandra* (1969).

Bennett, Daphne, *King Without a Crown, Albert Prince Consort of England 1819-1861* (1977).

Bennett, Daphne, *Vicky Princess Royal of England and German Empress* (1971).

Benson A.C. et al (ed.), *Letters of Queen Victoria 1837-1901* 1st series (1907), 2nd series (1926), 3rd series (1930).

Benson, E. F., *Daughters of Queen Victoria* (1939).

Bentley, Nicholas, *The Victorian Scene* (1968).

Boase, Frederick, *Modern English Biography* (1901).

Brown, Ivor, *Balmoral, The History of a Home* (1955).

Cecil, Lord David, *Lord M. or The Later Life of Lord Melbourne* (1954).

Connell, Brian, *Regina v. Palmerston* (1962).

Duff, David, *Alexandra, Princess and Queen* (1979).

Esher, Viscount (ed.), *The Girlhood of Queen Victoria, A Selection of Her Majesty's Diaries Between the Years 1832 & 1840* (1912).

Eyck, Frank, *The Prince Consort, A Political Biography* (1959).

Fulford, Roger (ed.), *Darling Child: The Private Correspondence of Queen Victoria and the Crown Princess of Prussia, 1871-1878* (1976).

– *Dearest Child: Letters between Queen Victoria and the Princess Royal 1858-1861* (1964).

– *Dearest Mama: Letters between Queen Victoria and the Crown Princess of Prussia, 1861-1864* (1968).

– *Your Dear Letter: Private Correspondence of Queen Victoria and the Crown Princess of Prussia, 1865-1871* (1971).

– *Royal Dukes, Queen Victoria's 'Wicked Uncles'* (1948).

Hatch, Alden, *The Mountbattens* (1965).

Healey, Edna, *Lady Unknown, The Life of Angela Burdett-Coutts* (1978).

Holt, Edgar, *Plon-Plon, The Life of Prince Napoleon 1822-891* (1973).

Illustrated London News 1866-1897.

Kinloch Cooke, C., *H.R.H. Princess Mary Adelaide Duchess of Teck* (1900).

Kurtz, Harold, *The Empress Eugénie* (1964).

Longford, Elizabeth, *Victoria R.I.* (1976).

Paget, Lady Walburga, *In My Tower* (1924).

Ponsonby, Sir Frederick (ed.), *Letters of The Empress Frederick* (1928).

Pope-Hennessy, James, *Queen Mary* (1959).

St Aubyn, Giles, *The Royal George* (1963).

Sophie, Queen, 'Letters of Queen Sophie of The Netherlands to Lady Malet 1840-1877', unpublished MS, Duke University Library, North Carolina.

Sudley, Lord (ed.), *The Lieven-Palmerston Correspondence 1828-1856* (1943).

The Times (London), 1830-1897.

Willis, G.M., *Ernest Augustus Duke of Cumberland & King of Hanover* (1954).

Woodham Smith, Cecil, *Florence Nightingale 1820-1910* (1950).

Index

Kensal . 1744. 12 Oct